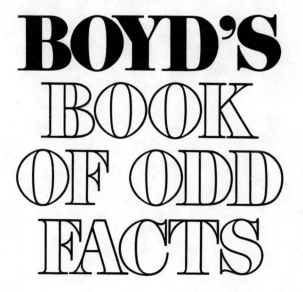

BOYD'S BOOK OF ODD FACTS

BOYD'S
BOOK
OF ODD
FACTS

By L. M. BOYD

Illustrated by Alex Chin

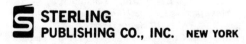

STERLING
PUBLISHING CO., INC.   NEW YORK

Oak Tree Press Co., Ltd.
London & Sydney

For Patricia

Compiled by Sheila Anne Barry

Copyright © 1979 by L. M. Boyd
Published by Sterling Publishing Co., Inc.
Two Park Avenue, New York, N.Y. 10016
Distributed in Australia by Oak Tree Press Co., Ltd.,
P.O. Box J34, Brickfield Hill, Sydney 2000, N.S.W.
Distributed in the United Kingdom by Ward Lock Ltd.,
116 Baker Street, London W.1
Manufactured in the United States of America
All rights reserved
Library of Congress Catalog Card No.: 78-66296
Sterling ISBN 0-8069-0166-7 Trade   Oak Tree 7061-2612-2
0167-5 Library

Contents

1 You Heard It Right

HELLO

Just about every national group has its own way of saying "Hello." "Rejoice" is the greeting of the Greeks. The Hebrews say, "Peace." The Dutch traditionally say, "May you have a hearty dinner." The Germans say, "How goes it?" The Poles say, "Are you happy?" The Chinese ask, "Is your stomach in order?" But I like the way the Moors historically delivered their how-do-you-do's. They rode full tilt down on you, stopped suddenly, then fired a pistol over your head. That's class.

COFFEE. The record shows that Persian Sultan Selim I hanged two doctors simply because they advised him to stop drinking so much coffee.

Wagner's music is better than it sounds.

Bill Nye

CHIMPS. Dr. Geoffrey H. Bourne of the Yerkes Primate Research Center said this: "We once had a chimp who could sort photographs of apes and human beings into two piles. Apes on one pile, humans on the other. But peculiarly, every time she got to her own picture, she put it on the pile with the human beings."

Loaded dice were found in the ruins of Pompeii.

LATE ARRIVALS

The dry truth is the word Christmas didn't turn up until the year A.D. 1038.

It's also true that the Irish city of Dublin was founded about A.D. 840 by Norwegians.

Maybe you know the gourmet delicacy known as pâté de foie gras is made from the enlarged livers of well-fattened geese. But do you know how those geese get well-fattened? Women in Eastern Europe force feed the birds by pushing potato dumplings down their throats with their fingers. Chet L. Switell told me that.

CLASSIFIED. Looks as though everybody has some favorite classified ad. Friend Robert John Allen says his is: "Personals: To the party who stole the unattended lawnmower from my front yard: I hope, when you arrived home, that your mother ran out from underneath the porch, barked at you, and bit you on the leg."

RED SCENT. Why the perfume makers in the Soviet Union have not yet successfully competed in the worldwide markets may be suggested by the fact that one of their recently exported scents was named "Black Casket."

Best-selling canned soup in the People's Republic of China is labeled "White Fungus."

Peculiarity about some tongue twisters is they're fairly easy to say once, but exceedingly difficult to say twice in a rapid manner. If you can handle this one repeatedly, consider yourself a thuperior thpeaker: "Sinful Caesar sipped his snifter, seized his knees and sneezed."

The growers of silk worms in Spain reportedly play castanet music to the little beasts on the theory it will stimulate silk production.

TWINS

It's possible for a woman to bear twins, each of whom is the offspring of a different father; medical men agree to that.

Twins have been born as much as a month apart.

DOCTORS. The numerous medical malpractice suits are said to have prompted that bumper sticker seen of late on doctors' cars: "Feeling sick? Call your lawyer."

WOLFESS? Please note, the leader of a wolf pack is always a she.

Were you aware that ants won't cross a white chalk line?

In railroad lingo, if the train runs south, it's described as westbound, but if it runs north, it's described as eastbound. Curious.

Q. The moon is receding from the earth, it's reported. By how much?

A. About half an inch (13 mm) a year.

COMPUTERS. Some computers have been known to catch cold. One in California, for instance, recently shut itself down until its operator started covering it every night with an electric blanket.

Q. What's cataplexy?

A. A rare ailment that paralyzes its victims when they try to laugh.

The bridges across the Mississippi River are at their shortest in winter. In midsummer, they're all several inches longer.

First man ever to domesticate a horse did that thing not to ride the beast, but milk it. Or so numerous experts contend.

Am advised that yaks give pink milk.

The government of India wanted to put together some statistical data about manufacturing companies there. So it sent out a questionnaire to managers. One of the queries was: "How many people do you employ, broken down by sex?"

THE TRUTH ABOUT DOVES. Bird authorities claim that emblem of peace called the dove can be a vicious little monster. It's merciless, they say, when pecking an opponent to death.

10

Man is the only animal who'll eat with an enemy.

Imagine you've read about the famous golden apples of Greek mythology. They were apricots.

PROVERBS

Cervantes was the fellow who defined the proverb as a short sentence derived from long experience.

Our Language man has started a collection of reconditioned proverbs, like: "A house divided makes many apartments." And "If at first you don't succeed, try a little ardor." And "A bird in the hand is finger-lickin' good." Others will follow.

That terrier known as the Kerry Blue is always born black.

A memo put out by the National Travel Association of Denmark translates: "The official rate of tipping in Denmark is 12½ per cent, but 15 per cent insures better service, so most people give 17 per cent."

THERE'S NO ACCOUNTING ... Although Napoleon Bonaparte reportedly bathed daily, history records he insisted his Josephine not do so.

FIRST THINGS FIRST. Rule No. 1 in Miss Leslie's Behavior Book of 1853 reads, "Do not eat in mittens."

In Rumford, Maine, it's against the law to bite your landlord.

LOS ANGELES

Los Angeles law prohibits the hanging out in public view of ladies' lingerie.

What other town besides Los Angeles can you name that employs a professional skunk hunter?

A Florida land developer with 114 vacant lots for sale advertises his Sunday tours as "The Greatest Earth on Show."

SEE?

Just about one out of every 166 people has such bad eyesight that said party can't read a story in an ordinary newspaper even with glasses.

It has been noted that the effect your glasses have on your vision depends on what you drink out of them.

Certainly you knew that blood is thicker than water, but did you know it's exactly six times thicker than water?

Among those patients who survive heart attacks, the overweight victims generally live longer than the slim ones. Why? The medicos say they don't know yet.

Everybody knows that item of feminine apparel known as bloomers was named after Amelia Bloomer. But few know that she absolutely refused to put on a pair of those things in her last 35 years of life.

This is the last verse of a famous poem: *"And you each gentle animal / to you for life may bind / and make it follow at your call / if you are always kind."* Can you name the poem? Of course, of course, "Mary Had a Little Lamb."

Until about 50 years ago, babies in Finland were delivered in saunas, the historians report.

MOSQUITOES. Those medical specialists who study diseases such as malaria still insist the bite of a mosquito is potentially more dangerous than the bite of a tarantula.

Q. Wasn't it Will Rogers who wrote, "Reader, suppose you were an idiot; and suppose you were a member of Congress; but I repeat myself."?

A. No, that was Mark Twain. Twain also said: "More than one cigar at a time is excessive smoking." And: "Nothing helps the scenery like ham and eggs."

I'm told the artists' finest paint brushes are made from the eyelashes of camels.

BIG BIRD. One egg of that extinct fowl known as the elephant bird could have made an omelet big enough to feed 90 people.

The cockroach has been on earth approximately 364 times longer than man.

BOOM! Amazing the oddball things that have exploded quite violently. Freshly mined diamonds have done so. So have elephant tusks when refrigerated. And touched off with sparks, the dust of dried milk has blown up warehouses.

2 Male and Female

This character got into a fight with his girlfriend. So he wrote her a note: "I sure am sorry to be so forgetful. I know I proposed to you the other night, but I can't remember if you said yes or no." She wrote back: "I was really pleased to hear from you. I knew I'd said no to somebody the other night, but I'd forgotten who." The foregoing is Item No. 1764-C in our Love and War man's file labeled "Engagements, Broken."

Were you aware that the sort of light a pumpkin gets in its infancy determines its sex? What, you didn't even know that pumpkins are male or female? Yes, indeed.

It's the female horsefly, not the male, who bites the horse. And the male cockroach is known to be smarter than the female.

Noted psychiatrist and author Theodor Reik: "One might observe a couple walking down the street talking. You will usually find that the man looks ahead, but rarely looks at the woman while she speaks. Yet she'll often glance at him out of the corner of her eye. This quick glance through half-closed eyes is rarely observed in men, but frequently in women."

14

Q. At what age do young girls grow the least in height? How about young boys?

A. Girls, from age 9 to 10. Boys, from age 10 to 11. With numerous exceptions.

After two snails mate, they both lay eggs. Now that's equal rights.

It's a simple medical fact that far more girls than boys grow up knock-kneed.

Among some African tribesmen, the affectionate thing for a fellow to do when he greets his girlfriend is blow on her hand and then rub her on the right ear. Our Love and War man says that's equivalent there to a kiss. Bear in mind, this is not the same African tribesman who shows affection by sticking his tongue out at his girlfriend while smacking her on the stomach.

Tests show girls' memories are better than boys'.

LEFT-HANDED. A scholar who has made a study of genes contends left-handed mothers are more likely than left-handed fathers to produce left-handed children.

FICKLE FEMALES? Studies by Dr. Karl F. Robinson of Northwestern University reportedly prove that men change their minds two or three times more often than do women.

An annual report of the New York Opticians' Association noted: "Whether men make passes at girls who wear glasses depends a lot on their frames."

The first printing of the Soviet Union's party-line brochure on sex education sold out in three hours.

If music can make you weep, chances are 99 to one you're not a woman but a man, studies show. Rarely is any woman moved to tears by a melody. But numerous are the men so susceptible.

Funny thing about the kangaroo. Once the female is adult, she can be said to have gained her full growth. But that male goes on growing as long as he lives.

Q. Is the human heart as heavy as a pound of butter?

A. Half as heavy among women, usually. Maybe three-fourths as heavy among big men.

Medical men say only about 5 per cent of the human body differs between the male and the female.

GENDER MYSTERIES

Why girls get about five times as many warts as do boys remains a mystery, yes?

And why twice as many men as women fall out of hospital beds is another mystery.

Most Swedish butchers are men, most Finnish butchers are women. Shrug.

Looks as though no further argument is possible against the old line that men are more "red blooded" than women. They are. A man has far more red corpuscles than a woman of the same weight and height.

CLIMBERS. Veteran forest rangers in frequent contact with mountain climbing parties say women tend to have better endurance than men. The women don't seem to be affected as quickly by the short supply of oxygen in the high altitudes, they report.

KNITTING. In the days of King Henry VIII, knitting was the specialty of men, not women.

If a woman is to commit murder, odds run three out of four she'll do that thing in her own home, most probably in her kitchen. If a man commits murder in his home, he's most apt to do it in the bedroom.

SIGN LANGUAGE. Can you think of any mammal that does not tend to cock its head slightly when it hears something of interest? Neither can I. Our Love and War man says both women and men use it instinctively to impress members of the opposite sex. They send out a signal that says, in effect, "What you're telling me is fascinating." Even as you can tell a lie by shaking your head and nodding it, so can you lie by tipping it. Head-tipping can be exceedingly sneaky.

When a man buys flowers, if ever, he tends to pick red. A woman, though, is inclined to go for pink. Or blue. Or whatever off-hue is at hand. A survey among florists reveals this.

It is the woman over age 55, not the man, who is most inclined to speak charitably of her enemies. Or so a lengthy study of such matters indicates. That was the same study which purported to prove that men over age 55 are the greatest animal lovers.

Most bathroom tile is so constituted that it resonates to the lower bass and baritone notes, but not to the higher soprano tones. That's said to be why many men but few women sing in the bathtub.

Far more women than men break bones on skis.

DISCRIMINATION? The notion that a newspaper's classified ads must not be categorized under "male" and "female" is embarrassingly idiotic. At least a Salt Lake City advertiser must think so. In the *Deseret News* classified, he inserted: "Man or woman to work in advertising agency, making razor blade commercials. Must have heavy beard." And: "Pregnant man or woman to model maternity clothes."

FIRST IMPRESSIONS

When a man sees a girl he has never seen before, what's the first thing he notices about her? Pollsters put that query to numerous military men. Her figure, said 25 per cent. Her disposition, 19 per cent. Her manners, 18 per cent. Her face, 16 per cent. Her style, 8 per cent. Her voice, 7 per cent. Her hair, 7 per cent. Please note, our Love and War man says the foregoing findings list the first thing noticed, not the most significant thing. As previously reported, most significant to the man when he notices the girl is whether the girl notices him.

It has been proved that women, when deliberating in jury rooms, do not talk anywhere nearly as much as men.

Women can talk longer with less effort than can men. That has been proved repeatedly. Why? Because the vocal cords of women are shorter than those of men and so release less air through them to carry the sound. Matter of breathing.

Among parrots, though, it is the male that's the best talker. In fact, the female hardly talks at all. Echolalia is what the science boys call parrot talk. That's the word for the repetition of noises without any understanding of what they mean.

It has been scientifically proved that a woman gets drunk more quickly than a man, even though she and he be the same weight and put away exactly the same amount of alcohol. The why of this is noteworthy. A woman's body is about 60 per cent water, give or take a little. A man's body is about 70 per cent water, with variations. So a man dilutes his booze just a little more than a woman does.

Another small physical difference between the average woman and man is her lips tend to be slightly larger and fleshier than his. Oh, you'd noticed?

Item No. 1876B in our Love and War man's file labeled "Broken Engagements" reads: "I knew my girlfriend and I were all washed up when she put my photograph in the bottom of her bird cage."

A team of medical experts in Virginia contends you're more likely to catch the common cold viruses by shaking hands than by kissing.

19

MERMAIDS?

The manatee is not a pretty critter. Lives in the sea. Shaped like a sack. Sunken eyes. Bristly moustache. Fat upper lip. A tail like a spade. Grows about 15 feet (4.5 m) long. Weighs a ton (.9 metric ton). And measures more than 7 feet (2.1 m) around the waist. That monstrosity is thought to have inspired among ancient sailors the earliest notions about beautiful mermaids. Those old boys must have been out on the water a long time, what?

Consider the index finger and the ring finger on your left hand, please. Which is the longer? Medical scholars who have made a study of the matter say the ring finger is longer than the index among six out of every ten men, but only three out of every ten women.

Residents of nudist colonies always wear clothes at their dances, I'm told.

WOMAN'S WORK ...

At last report, women's liberation had not yet come to the world's southernmost people, the Yahgan Indians of Tierra del Fuego. Boys aren't taught to swim. Girls are. Spear fishing is what the Yahgans do best. The man sits in the bow of the canoe. The woman in the stern paddles. Whenever it's necessary for somebody to go overboard—to wrestle with a speared seal, to retrieve a weapon, to tow the canoe through rocky waterways—it's the woman. Should mention, the seawater around there is the coldest that people have endured anywhere as a matter of custom.

Do you realize the average single woman puts in more years on the job than the average man? She can expect to work 45 years, he only 43.

To that long list of memorable fluffs by radio announcers, add this phrasing, delivered ad lib by a disc jockey in a laundry commercial: "Ladies who care to drive by and drop off their clothes will receive our special attention."

Q. Just how common is that thing called jealousy?

A. Mighty common, studies show. More than 96 per cent of a sizable sampling told surveyors recently that they'd experienced jealousy within the last six months.

All the women in this world put together weigh just about 85 per cent as much as all the men.

Q. Who is the more apt to have curly hair, a man or a woman?

A. Neither. Curly hair is impartial. Studies now show it's a toss-up.

Pollsters report they've learned that most young girls have their first romantic experiences in the homes of their boyfriends.

It was the official agency known as the U.S. Bureau of Standards that determined a woman's average reaction time behind the wheel of a car was nine to ten times swifter than a man's.

Suppose it's appropriate enough that the European oyster off the coast of Denmark changes its sex from male to female and back again just about every five years.

3 Money Money Money

Q. Who said: "When you have money in your pocket, you are wise and you are handsome and you sing well, too."? Ogden Nash?

A. No, that's an old Yiddish proverb. Ogden Nash said: "Oh, money, money, money, I am not necessarily one of those who thinks thee holy. But I often stop to wonder how thou can'st go out so fast when thou comest in so slowly."

What would you be willing to do for $1,000,000? Pollsters put that query to numerous citizens. Would you take off your clothes in public? Yes, said 12 per cent of those asked. Would you serve a year's jail term on a framed charge? Yes, said 13 per cent. Interesting. Those who would go to jail for a year outnumber those who would take off their clothes in public. In this survey, at any rate.

GOLD

More than 30 patents have been issued on inventions designed to extract gold from seawater.

Maybe you didn't know that your hair, if any, contains gold. Just 430 parts per billion, to be exact.

Q. What did we say before we came out with: "If you've got it, flaunt it"?

A. How about: "Them that has them, wears them." That was Diamond Jim Brady's line in reference to the 20,000 diamonds he owned. He sported batches of them all the time. Yes, they were real. Just one of his sets, containing 2,548 diamonds and rubies, would sell for more than $1 million now.

This week's favorite classified ad reads: "Special Notices: Join the Inflation Fighters Club. Yearly dues only $25 $50 $100."

Q. How much money did Henry Winkler get in the early days of the *Happy Days* show? How much later?

A. Then, about $750 per episode. Later, an estimated $80,000 per episode plus a cut of the profit.

Only U.S. currency in popular circulation that wasn't counterfeited by the Nazis during World War II was the $2 bill.

ONE WAY TO GET A LOAN. That old contention that bankers are heartless doesn't hold up. Take the case of Wendy Westfall, for instance. She was a teller at the First National Bank of Scotia. Lawmen took her by arm, though, charging her with embezzlement, and the court put her on probation for two years. The bank then gave her a four-year loan to repay the money.

FILTHY LUCRE. Microscopic examination of coins and currency proves such lucre is filthy. What, you know that? But do you know exactly how filthy? Drs. Derel L. Abrams and Norton G. Waterman of the University of Louisville School of Medicine undertook this study. And 13 per cent of the metal money and 42 per cent of the bills they tested proved to be germy. Very germy. They recommend we do business henceforth with $100 bills only. Such aren't handled so much. How true.

23

Biggest moneymaker for the Las Vegas casinos is craps, the game that gives the players the best odds.

The world's most popular board game, *Monopoly,* is banned in the Soviet Union.

VALUABLE ANIMALS

Q. What are the most valuable animals in the world?

A. Race horses, giant pandas and killer whales.

Q. Name the first race horse ever to win $1 million.

A. Citation. Passed the million mark in 1951.

Mister, has it ever occurred to you to let your wife negotiate your salary? If not, why not? That renowned columnist of yesteryear, O. O. McIntyre, did that. Largely because he chose not to get into a high-pressure hassle with his syndicators. The great Albert Einstein did likewise when he went to work for Princeton. However, McIntyre personally okayed the final deal. Einstein didn't even bother to ask what his income was.

The real meat in a typical frozen TV dinner actually costs you about $10 per pound. Or so say the experts who've thawed, weighed and calculated such grub.

PONY EXPRESS. History now takes little note that the financial backers of the renowned Pony Express dropped $200,000 in that 18-month operation.

Money is like a sixth sense—and you can't make use of the other five without it.

Somerset Maugham

ABUSED WORDS. The three most abused words in retail advertisements, according to a Better Business Bureau official, are "selling elsewhere for."

Here's a job offer for you. It's to last only 30 days. Starting pay is one cent per day. But the pay will double with each succeeding day. What, you won't take it? Too bad! That 30 days' work would get you $10,738,418.23.

World's currency most difficult to counterfeit is said to be that of Japan. Believe it's the special paper.

Q. Among the unmarried millionaires in the U.S.A., which outnumber which, the men or the women?

A. The women. By far. There are said to be 27,000 such ladies each with a net worth of at least $1 million. There are known to be only 11,000 men with that much wealth. Don't ask me where they are, exactly. Can only report most of them live in California, Texas, New York, Pennsylvania, Illinois and Ohio.

Remarkable how many millionaires went broke several times before they hit the big money for keeps. Take William Wrigley, Jr. Understand he went broke no less than four times before

25

his chewing gum money stuck. Once, he lost everything trying to sell umbrellas.

Not widely known is the fact that the famous steamboat builder Robert Fulton made so much money painting portraits in his teens that he was able to buy a farm for his mother.

SCOTS. A surveytaker recently canvassed numerous financial experts in Europe to learn they generally regarded the Scottish bankers as the best of the professional money managers.

IN THE WIND. So you still want to make $1 million, do you? All right, set up a company to manufacture water well windmills. Only one such firm now exists in this country, I'm told. But what with the energy shortage, numerous crafty citizens think they can convert those windmills to generate electricity. Orders for them are pouring in. As technology develops, the demand is expected to become explosive.

Ever pan for gold? Fascinating pastime, that. It's the claim of some mineralogists that your chances of striking a fine vein today are even greater than were the chances of the early California prospectors. Credit better maps.

Those proverb-prone Spanish say, "A dog with money is addressed as Mr. Dog."

Q. What proportion of working wives earn more money than do their husbands?

A. Three out of twenty.

HALLELUJAH! It was because Handel needed the money so quickly that he shut himself up for 21 days to write "The Messiah."

Q. Remember the late Coco Chanel, the fancy French lady of perfume fame? How much money did she make?

A. About $13,500 a week. Or so report the estimators. Incidentally, she never did own controlling interest in that perfume company. But she made a deal to collect 2 per cent royalty on every bottle of perfume called Chanel whatever. Did you know that during her entire 65 years as a Paris designer she never once used the color green?

PAUL REVERE

It was not for nothing that Paul Revere rode through the night, crying, "The British are coming!" He billed the Massachusetts State House 10 pounds 4 shillings to cover his expenses. That was the equivalent to $23.59 at this writing. He collected it, too.

Am asked the name of Paul Revere's favorite horse. Sorry. Nothing in that bulky batch of Revere's private papers indicates he ever owned a horse.

Could any one human being carry a million $1 bills? Not without a fair-sized truck. They'd weigh pritnear a ton (0.9 tonne) and fill up 42 cubic feet (1.3 cubic meters) of space.

4 Names and Faces

PALINDROME

No other palindrome, a message which spells alike both front-ward and backward, is as long as this one, I'll warrant: "Dennis, Nell, Edna, Leon, Nedra, Anita, Rolf, Nora, Alice, Carol, Leo, Jane, Reed, Dena, Dale, Basil, Rae, Penny, Lana, Dave, Denny, Lena, Ida, Bernadette, Ben, Ray, Lila, Nina, Jo, Ira, Mara, Sara, Mario, Jan, Ina, Lily, Arne, Bette, Dan, Reba, Diane, Lynn, Ed, Eva, Dana, Lynne, Pearl, Isabel, Ada, Ned, Dee, Rena, Joel, Lora, Cecil, Aaron, Flora, Tina, Arden, Noel and Ellen sinned." Must have been some party, what?

Hardly anybody knows the first and middle names, Anna Mathilda, of one of the world's most famous women, Whistler's Mother.

Q. Why is "Mexico" so called?

A. Comes from *Mexitili*, the name of an Aztec god.

Am advised the name of Iowa comes from the Indian word Ayuhwa *meaning "sleepy ones."*

The names Kuznetsky in Russian, Kowalski in Polish, and Kovacs in Czech all translate into English as just plain Smith.

The name "Fraser" originally in France meant "hairdresser."

Q. Where's "Last Chance Gulch"?

A. That used to be the name of Montana's capital, Helena.

Had occasion the other day to put through a call to a newspaper publisher named Jonathan Segal. A most cordial gentleman. But the telephone operator broke up. Couldn't handle it. Giggled all the way through the switchboard. Ever since that pilot wrote that book about that bird, I gathered from Mr. Segal, people have been asking him if he's taking flying lessons.

Q. What's Redd Foxx's real name?

A. "Sanford," sir, "John Elroy Sanford."

The late Mama Cass Elliott started out as Ellen Naomi Cohen.

DO YOU KNOW . . . ?

How many women have you known by the name of Elizabeth? If you can't think of at least seven, you must've lived the life of a hermit. Or so says our Name Game man. He also reckons you've probably known seven men named Robert. And at least five girls and five boys named Carol and James, respectively. Those are the statistical odds among acquaintances, at any rate.

If a birth registrar in West Germany doesn't like the name a pair of parents give their newborn offspring, he can simply

29

refuse to register it. It happens, too. In Munich, a registrar declined to permit a couple to name their daughter Kai Beatrice. Kai was a man's name, he said. In Munster, a registrar refused to let parents name their daughter Kristin. That was a Norwegian name, he said, not a German name. In Schladern, a registrar wouldn't allow a father of Italian descent to call his son Pier Andrea. He said Andrea was a girl's name unfit for a German boy.

Here's a limerick sent along by Whitley H. Harris:

> *A Du Pont chemist from Destor*
> *Was known to be quite a jester.*
> *   When his wife with a smile*
> *   Said, "I'm expecting a child!"*
> *He replied, "She'll be named Polly Esther."*

I'll wager a stogie you can't name William Shakespeare's three brothers. Neither could I. Research reveals they were Gilbert, Richard and Edmund.

Add to that list of candidates for membership in the Proper Job Club: Susan Book, a librarian in Helena, and Dale Dye, Ravalli county coroner, both of Montana.

Did you realize that one out of every 59 persons in the U.S.A. is a Kelley?

Told you about those twins named War and Peace, but failed to mention the brother and sister in New York City named Dusk and Dawn.

Whale steak is served in one Boston restaurant, which offers, and indeed it ought, one of same free to any citizen who can prove his name is Jonah.

Albert, Harry, Frank and Henry are not the most common names of all for men. But they are among the 18 most common. And scholars who have made a study of the matter say they are the four among those most common 18 that are least liked.

Were you aware that Dr. Kissinger's real name is Heinz, not Henry?

WHAT WOULD YOU WRITE? When offered new pens to try out, 97 out of every 100 people write their own names. So reports a pen salesman.

Q. Where does Anthony rank now among the 10 most popular names for boys?

A. It's No. 6. Right after No. 5, Steven, and just before No. 7, William.

Old warrior chiefs in ancient England used to pick out special-duty soldiers by tapping their toughest fighters on the helmets. Each so tapped was called a "william." That's where the name came from, says our Language man.

Q. Where does Williams or Williamson rank on that list of this country's most popular surnames?

A. No. 3. Anybody named Smith or Johnson can tell you what No. 1 and No. 2 are.

MANNA?

It was in 1904 that C. W. Post tossed onto the market a brand of corn flakes he called "Elijah's Manna." Men of the cloth didn't like that name. How dare he associate his newfangled grub with God's gift to the children of Israel? For one thing, Elijah was served bread and meat, not manna. But that wasn't the point. Post repackaged his delicacy under the new name of "Post Toasties."

If you can't count at least 15 nicknames for Elizabeth, you're just not trying. No other Christian name has as many variations.

That famous Indian called *Geronimo* by the Mexicans was known earlier among his tribal compatriots as *Goyathlay* meaning "one who yawns."

Q. What was St. Patrick's real name?

A. Succat. He was a Frenchman.

Argument continues over the name of George Washington's favorite horse. Record at hand identifies the animal as "Blue Skin."

Again am asked the name of Jesse James' favorite horse. That one he called "Siroc."

Are you the possessor of one of these names? Alice, Bertha, Charles, David, Edward, Frank, George, Henry, Ira, James,

Kate, Louis, Mary, Nellie, Oliver, Peter, Quaker, Robert, Samuel, Thomas, Utah, Victor, X-ray, Young or Zebra? If so, you're listed in the telephone company's official spelling lesson for its operators. Those are its code names for the letters of the alphabet.

That word "hotdog" to describe a sausage cropped up first, not in the U.S., but in Europe in the 13th century, bear in mind.

That masculine moniker most frequently shed during the last 45 years in name-change actions by the courts is Adolph.

Note that Mildred is listed on one expert's roster of names most disliked by American women. Too bad, if true. Social Security rolls show it to rank No. 8 among the most widely used names of women. No. 9 among the most widely used names of men is Frank.

STRANGE NAMES

A researcher fascinated by funny feminine first names dug into the newspapers, phone books and college rosters to turn up the following girls' legal monikers: Dinette, Chlorine, Larceny, Blooma, Mecca. I like Larceny. Pretty ring to it. Almost as lyrical as Diarrhea. That, you may recall, was selected by a sizable sampling of first-graders as the most poetic feminine name of all.

Too many boys grow up with names they don't like. Believe the Indians had the right idea. They gave their offspring temporary names. To be changed for more satisfactory monikers after they'd proved themselves in their teen years. Crazy Horse, for example, started out as Curly. And Sitting Bull began as Jumping Badger.

TALLULAH. Girls named "Tallulah" like to think their moniker comes from a Cherokee word meaning "love maiden." That's a myth. The language boys say it comes from a Cherokee word meaning "terrible."

Those students of the mind who analyze doodles contend that a citizen who absentmindedly writes his or her own name as a matter of habit tends to lack confidence.

Q. Why is Nebraska called that?

A. Comes from the Oto Indian word *nebrathka* meaning "flat water."

It was two Algonquin Indian tribes, the Michi Gama and the Michi Sepe, that gave the names to the states of Michigan and Mississippi.

PREJUDICE

Scholars in San Diego asked 80 elementary school teachers to grade eight essays written by fifth and sixth grade students. The essays were just average, neither particularly good nor especially bad, but pretty much equal in quality. The tricky part of the report is that said scholars changed the names of the essay writers to phony monikers. Four were labeled with the names David, Michael, Karen and Lisa. And four were labeled Elmer, Hubert, Adelle and Bertha. Upshot: The essays that the teachers thought were written by David, Michael, Karen and Lisa scored one grade higher than those which they believed had been written by Elmer, Hubert, Adelle and Bertha. Teachers are indeed prejudiced by names, it seems.

R.I.P. And there are those, too, who collect tombstone epitaphs, as follows: "Owen Moore has gone away; owing more than he could pay." "Here lies the body of Lester Moore; four slugs from a .44; no less, no more." "Here lies the body of Jonathan Blake; he stepped on the gas instead of the brake." Any others?

5 Happy Dreams

Q. What are the chances of hitting a jackpot in a slot machine that's not rigged in favor of the house?

A. About one in 2,000.

A physical culture expert contends your best sleep comes when you lie without a pillow flat on your back with your feet apart and your hands palms up at your sides. Maybe so, don't know. However, it's common knowledge that's also the position in which you're most likely to snore. Did I tell you the best cure for snoring? Sew an empty thread spool in the middle of the back of your pajamas.

Wild animals don't snore.

A relatively recent ordinance in Dunn, North Carolina, out-laws snoring. At least loud snoring. And any citizen there who shakes up a neighborhood with such an offense can be jailed for a day or two.

SWALLOWS

Do you ever swallow while asleep? You do. Exactly 7.6 times per hour, if average. Dr. Clement S. Lear of the Harvard

School of Dental Medicine in Boston found that out. He also discovered you swallow 48 times while eating a 10-minute lunch, 34 times during one hour reading a fairly dull novel, and 31 times an hour just lying awake wondering why you can't doze off. More about swallows will be forthcoming as the demand warrants.

Researchers think that about four million people in this country get up every night to go for a little walk in their sleep.

A sign posted in the lobby of an English hostel reads: "Americans are requested to retire before 2 a.m. Germans are requested to arise no earlier than 6 a.m. Italians are requested to refrain from singing after 10 p.m."

How people got around to sleeping in pajamas, I do not know. Can only report they were not originally intended to be sleeping attire. They were first used in India as lounging costumes.

Don't forget, diamonds have been found in meteorites, sir.

Q. Do elephants sleep much?

A. Maybe two or three hours a night.

INSOMNIA. Sleep specialists recommend either of two activities to prevent insomnia. One, a 15-minute walk. Two, a 10-minute soaking of the feet in hot water. Either, just before bedtime. Both are said to tease the blood away from the brain into the lower extremities, thus inhibiting the mental action that makes for wakefulness.

Understand there's a tricky lamp shade out now constructed in such a manner that the rising heat from the light bulb activates a sort of slow-motion picture of a yawning face. Insomniacs are urged to buy. The maker says nothing else but drugs can so rapidly bring on sleep.

What, the knock-knock jokes are back? So a juvenile today reports. It was 1935, I believe, when they first popped up. Then there was a revival of them about 10 years ago. Last one that comes to mind went: "Knock knock." "Who's there?" "Highway cop." "Highway cop who?" "Highway cop every morning with a headache."

Unmarried women dream more in their sleep than do married women. All women in general dream more than do men. And youthful citizens dream more than do retired people. Or so contend the sleep researchers.

DAYDREAMS

That you tend to dream about every 90 minutes when you're asleep is not news. What's news is that you tend to dream about every 90 minutes when you're awake, too. Researchers in Washington University at St. Louis found that out. Your daydreams, they claim, are just about as regular as your sleep dreams, surprisingly.

If you average 50 m.p.h. (80 km per hour) on a car trip for 10 hours, you can figure you'll drive 42 miles (67 km) with your eyes closed. Blinking is why.

No, Joan of Arc was not really burned at the stake as the legend goes, but was sent to prison in Rouen in 1431. Or such is the claim of members of France's Armoises Family. They say they have documents to prove it. After Joan's release, they contend, she married one Robert des Armoises. And the couple lived near Metz.

ZEBRAS. Zebras in a herd never all sleep at the same time. Always there are a few lookouts.

TWIN BEDS

That it was the great British furniture designer Thomas Shera-ton who originated the first twin beds has been widely reported. Not so widely known, however, is the fact that twin beds were originally created for use only in extremely hot summer weather. The record indicates Sheraton had no intention whatsoever at the outset of selling such furniture to people who didn't live in castles.

When an elderly couple chooses twin beds, it's usually the man who makes the decision. But when a young couple buys twin beds, it's almost invariably the woman who so decides. Such is the contention of a bed salesman.

Q. Ideally, how much longer than the sleeper should the bed be?

A. At least 7 inches (18 cm), claim the bedmakers.

It's called "taresthesia" when your foot goes to sleep.

Trees sleep, too. At least, they require relief from light daily. Or so an authority on the matter reports.

POISON PROTECTION. The glass makers of Venice centuries ago spread the phony notion that contact with toxic substances would cause their crystal goblets to shatter. A mighty tricky sales technique, that one. Worldwide, but particularly in Europe, scared potentates, who controlled enough money to make a fair market, bought up that Venetian glassware in the belief it would protect them from poisoners.

Q. Do hippopotamuses ever bite people?

A. Certainly do. With fair frequency. Several hundred people a year in Africa get killed by hippos. Knocked out of boats. Drowned. Dragged under water. Or bitten to death.

HOW MUCH SLEEP DO YOU NEED?

Approximately 8 per cent of the grownups need no more than five hours of sleep each night. About 15 per cent need less than six hours. As many as 52 per cent need between seven and eight hours. And 15 per cent need as much as nine to 10 hours.

After age 20, the older you get, the less sleep you need, until age 60. Or so say researchers in Melbourne, Australia. Average 50-year-old man, they report, needs only 7 hours 15 minutes sleep per night.

Whether women actually need more sleep than do men is not the point. The point is they take more sleep—ordinarily, an average of 52 minutes more during each 24 hours—according to a recent survey.

As many as 100 pearls have been found in a single oyster.

The Black Plague killed around 25 million people in 1347. Victims developed round red rashes. Their pockets were stuffed with flowers in their final hours to camouflage the aroma of death. You've heard the nursery rhyme that goes "Ring around the rosies, pockets full of posies?" It dates all the way back to that Black Plague.

Q. Is it possible to learn a foreign language by use of tape recorded lessons while you sleep?

A. No, it's not possible. Or so some scientific tests indicate. A pair of California doctors wired 21 men to check out their brain waves. That showed whether they were just drowsy or deeply asleep. Records were played to them at five minute intervals. Upshot was they learned when drowsy, but not at all when soundly aslumber.

PAJAMA PARTY

If you want your mattress to last, invite your friends, neighbors and relatives to sleep on it. That's the peculiar advice of a mattress manufacturer. Each citizen, says he, sprawls in positions of habit when asleep. This sameness tends to wear out mattresses. But a variety of guests, all curled and stretched out in their own particular manners, allows the mattress to wear evenly, thus more slowly. Remember that. Dispatch invitations immediately. No, never mind the nonsense. But this manufacturer says the foregoing explains why hotel and motel mattresses hold up longer.

Sleep specialists say they now know for sure that birds dream.

Reported some time back that the left leg of the chicken tends to be tenderer than the right leg. The chicken sleeps on its right leg, thus developing tougher muscles, it's said. Now a Boise client wants to know who made this scientific discovery. A hotel chef named Pablo Sanzenis in Mexico City, that was the fellow. His standing order for dinner parties is to serve the guest of honor the left leg, always.

Those scholars who study dreams say two out of every five can be described as frightening if not terrifying.

Studies show whales, too, dream in their sleep.

What's responsible for the scientifically proved fact that a rabbit's ears go limp when it dreams?

Nonsmokers dream more.

FREEZING

Wasn't it Jack London who spread the notion that you must stay awake to stay alive in subzero Arctic weather? Think so. Lot of people still believe it. But it's wrong. Military experiments prove that. If you're dressed warmly, not wet, and bedded under cover from the wind, sleep is just about your best defense against the cold. Exhaustion is what leads to freezing death. Sleep tends to save the heat in you.

OUT LIKE A LIGHT. Sleep researchers contend it takes about seven minutes for the average citizen to doze off each night.

CAT AND MOUSE

Certainly you know all about the human mummies of ancient Egypt, but were you aware that thousands of cats and mice also were mummified then?

Is it instinctive for cats to catch mice? Always thought so, but research indicates otherwise. The science boys now say caged kittens will play with grown mice, but won't kill them unless taught to do so by older cats.

Hypnophobia, as you might guess, is the fear of going to sleep. And it's not so uncommon, really. Develops sometimes in a child, a mental specialist reports, when the parents wait for the youngster to doze off, then leave the house. If that child repeatedly wakes up to find it has been abandoned, even though temporarily, some degree of hypnophobia may set in.

INSOMNIA

When you have a little trouble getting to sleep, try letting the fingertips of one hand just barely touch the fingertips of the other hand for a while. A doctor who treats insomniacs says this simple technique works remarkably well.

An expert in Swedish massage reports he finally found an unfailing way to cure his insomnia. He stretches out face up on the floor, he says, with two tennis balls under the nape of his neck. Dozes right off, he says. Might try that, sir.

No doubt most mothers already know what Georgetown University researchers now say they're sure of, too. Namely, that babies get to sleep more quickly and stay asleep longer when they're put down on their stomachs instead of their backs.

March is said to be that month in which children sleep most soundly.

Growth. Children grow more while they're asleep than while they're awake.

That African butterfly known as the Patilio Antimachus with its 10-inch (25-cm) wing span is so filled with poison it will kill any leopard that eats it.

Q. Do insects sleep?

A. Sort of. They don't close their eyes. No eyelids. But they lie around and look dazed every so often.

Was reported that the porpoise sleeps with one eye open. Why? It has to surface every minute or so for air. That open eye keeps track of the size of the waves.

To his long list of fancy palindromes, our Language man has added, "Sex at noon taxes."

The medical experts who urge us to sleep on our right sides say their recommendation has nothing to do with the where-abouts of the heart. It's the digestive system that works better in that position, they report.

Sleep specialists say most people spend no more than 11 min-utes at a time in unbroken motionless slumber.

Sleep researchers also contend only about one person in twenty dreams in color.

CALORIES

It's highly likely you change your sleeping position between 30 and 40 times a night. Question arises if this causes you to burn up energy in your sleep. Some. But not much. You can expect to use up .043 calories per pound during an eight-hour sleep. Multiply that figure by your weight to get your calorie consumption while snoozing. At 190 pounds (86 kg), I'm sup-posed to expend only 8.17 calories. That's not enough. Going to have to get more sleep.

SNORING

Exactly 82 out of every 100 people who snore when asleep on their backs, stop that snoring when they turn on their sides, studies show.

That the overweight man is more apt to snore than the thin fellow is widely known. Flabby tissues are blamed, mostly. But there's another reason. When asleep, the fat man is likely to spend most of the night flat on his back with only an occa-sional roll from side to side. But the lightweight tends to sleep face down a lot, too. And you know how that stops the snoring.

The men who prefer to sleep on their backs outnumber the women who do so by four to one. Sleep studies at the Univer-sity of Florida prove that.

43

CATNAPS

A man of medicine claims it's actually possible for a long distance runner to catnap while in motion. And for an exhausted soldier to doze off while marching. And for an endurance swimmer intermittently to lose consciousness while in the water. What this medico means, it's assumed, is the brain can go to sleep without the body doing likewise.

The three most famous catnappers in world history were Thomas Edison, Winston Churchill and Mrs. Eleanor Roosevelt. Edison intermittently dozed on his workbench. Churchill dropped off from time to time in his desk chair. And Mrs. Roosevelt napped practically everywhere. In fact, once, after Norman Thomas delivered to a large Madison Square Garden audience an introduction of Mrs. Roosevelt as the featured speaker, he then had to shake her awake on stage so she could take the podium.

Was the claim of old Cedric Adams that the human brain during an eight-hour workday steals about 75 minutes in catnaps. With stenographers and managing editors, he said, it runs a little higher.

6 If the Oceans Went Dry

SALT. Question comes up as to how much salt we'd wind up with if all the oceans went dry. Government statisticians say enough to build a wall 18 miles (29 km) high, a mile thick, all the way around the earth at the equator. But there is no Federal grant to fund such a project at this time, surprisingly.

Ocean storms sink more than a hundred big ships a year. Even today. Wilted bodies drift down. Cluttered cargoes, too. The fierce winds and great waves pass. With some exceptions, you don't hear much about them. The owners wait, then file their insurance claims. They're not interested in publicizing their losses. The people who know about it all are the salvage men and Lloyd's of London.

Who was it that reported a shipload of yoyos sank in Manila Bay, but came back up 38 times?

Q. What's sleet?

A. A raindrop that bumps into a snowflake in midair where the temperature is below 32 degrees F. (0 degrees C.). They ice together.

You've heard the Antarctic year-round is the coldest place on earth. It's also the windiest.

CHRISTMAS TREES

The best Christmas trees need at least 140 hours of air temperatures below 40 degrees F. (4.4 degrees C.) before they're cut. That much cool weather produces a lasting green freshness, I'm told.

Q. Which kills more people, lightning or tornadoes?

A. Lightning. Over the years. Tornadoes do in about half as many citizens, but rack up a lot more property damage.

Claim now is that California's redwood trees started out in the Arctic. Scholars say they migrated. Took them 75 million years to make the trip. No, not by dog sled. Wind and weather pushed them south.

Now comes the report that the Sahara Desert is expanding south by about half a mile (.8 km) every year.

Is there such a thing as an average thundercloud? Must be, because weathermen say the average contains 100,000 tons (90,000 tonnes) of water.

WATER

Most all the world's water is saltwater. Just 97.137 per cent to be exact. About 2.24 per cent is ice and snow. Another .6129 per cent is underground. Figure .009 per cent is in freshwater lakes. Maybe .0001 per cent is in the rivers. And only .001 per cent is in the atmosphere. Got it? If this picture changes, expect a prompt report.

Q. You've heard the old saying, "Rainbow at night, sailors' delight, rainbow at morning, sailors take warning." What's the point?

A. When you face a rainbow, you're always situated between it and the sun with the sun at your back. Most rains move from west to east. So if you see the rainbow to the east in the evening when the sun is at your back, that suggests the storm is moving away from you. But if you see the rainbow to the west, the sun at your back, that suggests the storm is moving toward you.

The two most violent earthquakes ever recorded both centered underwater in the Pacific. One, on Jan. 31, 1906, broke about 200 miles (320 km) off the west coast of South America. The other, on March 2, 1933, hit off the east coast of Japan. No, they weren't the deadliest, just the most violent.

Q. How many active volcanoes are there, worldwide?

A. About 455 plus an estimated 80 more underwater.

Maybe you didn't realize there's a snowless valley right in the middle of Antarctica. About 4,000 square miles (10,400 square km) of it. Lake Vanda sits in the center. The lake's covered with ice, all right. But the water temperature down at the bottom is in the high 70 degrees F. (21 degrees C.).

47

Q. How thick is that ice over the Arctic Ocean?

A. Seven to 10 feet (2 to 3 m) in most places.

Q. How deep goes the ice at the South Pole?

A. About a mile and a half (2.4 km). Ground level there actually is 600 feet (180 m) below sea level. But that ice gives the place some altitude, even so. Which is why it's colder than the North Pole, incidentally.

SUNLIGHT

Which gets more sunlight over the course of a year, the North Pole, the equator or the South Pole? You're right, if you said the North Pole. There are 4,400 hours of daylight in a year at the equator, 4,500 hours at the North Pole and 4,380 at the South Pole.

No other nation worldwide gets as many tornadoes as the U.S.A.

FISH. Fish cough. And the more polluted the water, the more they cough. Finally realizing this, the environmental scientists are measuring water pollution by monitoring with sensitive instruments the coughing of fish. You're right, it's a federal project.

Were you aware that an estimated 20 million plastic bottles are floating around in the north Pacific?

The water that drains off Japan's Mt. Fuji is so polluted with alkaline that photographic negatives can be developed in it.

Q. What's the average temperature of the world?

A. 58 degrees F. (14.6 degrees C.).

BAD WATER

Beware of the crystal clear spring water where no bugs, worms or tadpoles crawl, where no algae breeds nor any moss grows upon the rocks around. Beware, beware. Such a place is Onion Springs, a waterhole northeast of Moab, Utah. It's got arsenic in it. It's not the water that's scummy with flora and fauna that's bad. It's the dead water. Remember that the next time you and your mule get lost.

Will you buy the claim that some fish can hear the sound of a worm wiggling on the bottom of a creek? Neither will I.

Did you ever watch the waves roll onto an ocean beach? Here's a fair technique to figure how fast they travel. Count the seconds between two arriving crests. Multiply by 3.5. For instance, if 10 seconds elapse between the first and second waves, they're rolling along at 35 m.p.h. (56 km per hour), count on it.

Q. Why doesn't anybody know even after all these years just how many islands there are in the Pacific?

A. Because a lot of the littler ones keep appearing and dis-appearing.

In Oklahoma, it's against the law to give liquor to fish.

The Yangtze River Valley of China and the Gulf Coast of the United States aren't precisely opposite one another on the earth, but almost. As previously reported, alligators have survived in these two places, but nowhere else worldwide. This is what so puzzles the lizard experts. The two spots could hardly be farther apart.

All porcupines float.

Q. Which is bigger, the Pacific Ocean or all the world's land acreage?

A. The Pacific. By 25 per cent.

Blame the coldness of the water for the fact that more fishermen drown in May than during any other month.

What's perfectly white? Nothing on earth, not even fresh snow, say the science boys.

Q. What's the U.S. Weather Bureau definition of a blizzard?

A. Has to be below 20 degrees F. (−6.7 degrees C.) with wind blowing more than 30 m.p.h. (48 km per hour). And snow flying. Not necessarily snow falling. It can be blowing heavily. There is such a thing as a blizzard without fresh snow.

Not many realize that the South Pole rarely gets more than five inches (12.5 cm) of new snow a year.

Can infrared rays pass through smog and clouds, water and glass? Smog and clouds, yes. Water and glass, no.

Little seals have to be taught how to swim.

Q. It's known that sea level differs from place to place in ocean to ocean. So at what point is sea level measured to get a norm?

A. It's determined locally, and each locality has its own unique conditions. Sea level seems to be rising around Alaska. But around Galveston, Texas, it appears to be sinking. Worldwide, it's said to be rising slightly, what with the ice caps melting a little.

It's said that anybody who is 80 years old most probably has walked a sufficient number of steps to travel six times around the earth.

The shorter a jackrabbit's ears, the colder the climate he lives in.

All 10 of the world's 10 coldest major cities are in the Soviet Union. And coldest of the lot is that Mongolian town called Ulan Bator.

Q. Does it ever get too cold to snow?

A. Never. Record shows that snow fell in Antarctica's Little America while the thermometer registered minus 65 degrees F. (18.3 degrees C.).

When a duck dives underwater, its heartbeat slows down immediately. To less than half as fast as normal. That's not so odd, though. It's how said duck conserves oxygen.

STEAM. Steam is invisible. Yes, sir. It is that. If you look at a boiling teakettle, you'll see maybe half an inch (13 mm) of space directly above the spout that looks perfectly clear. It's steam. The foggy gray above is made up of tiny beads of water that condense out of the steam.

SAINT BERNARD

The Saint Bernard dog of the Alps was pretty nifty in the rescue of lost climbers. That's widely known. But how could it see in those blinding blizzards? And how could it follow a scent over new-fallen snow? It couldn't. Not well, anyway. It relied on its ears, mostly. That dog's hearing is sensitive beyond belief.

Besides man, the only animal able to repeat music composed by people is the seal, don't forget.

52

Chinese scientists contend Mt. Everest is 26 feet (7.8 m) taller now than it was 100 years ago. The whimsical report suggests that anybody who wants to climb it better get started. It's still growing.

UNDERWATER? That there are mountains higher than Everest under the oceans is widely known. But were you aware there are also barren deserts underwater where no plant life grows?

Any ocean area with a depth of more than 18,000 feet (5400 m) is called a "deep." So far, more than 100 deeps have been charted. But hardly any are far out from land. Almost all are right next to mountainous islands.

KILLER WHALES. Client asks why the killer whale is so called. Inasmuch as there are only a few known instances wherein said beast ever killed anybody. In a school of fish, the animal kills its grub in fast succession, then swings back to eat the whole shebang. That's why.

Those Oklahoma legislators must have been feeling a bit whimsical the day they passed a law which prohibits the catching of whales in that state.

BIG BERG

There it goes, already northwest of South America's southern tip, heading toward Africa: an iceberg 36 times the size of Bermuda. Watchers aren't worried, though. They figure it will break up when it gets into warmer waters. Besides, it's not on a regular shipping lane. Still, an iceberg 36 times as big as Bermuda must be something to behold, what?

Q. How thick does the ice on the lake have to be to support the weight of a car? Of a man?

A. Car, about 8 inches (20 cm). Man, three or maybe four inches (7.5 or 10 cm).

Q. Is there really such a thing as a white Eskimo?

A. So it's said. Early in this century, Vilhjalmur Stefansson discovered a group of blond Eskimos on Victoria Island. Descendants of Viking colonists mated to natives, it's thought.

When the temperature drops, dress a little on the light side, not too heavily. That has long been the advice of the Eskimos. Claim is if you feel cool, you're all right. But if you bundle up enough to perspire, you're done for.

Q. How do you account for the fact that there's never any fat on a shark steak?

A. A shark stores all its fat in its liver. And speaking of sharks, did you know the white shark never gets sick? And it's immune to cancer.

Only fish that can blink both eyes is the shark.

Q. How can the Peruvians grow things around Lima if it never rains there?

A. A fog bank hangs over the city about six months out of every year. It's called the *garua*. Dampens things down fairly well.

India's Ganges River starts out in an ice cave 10,300 feet (3,090 m) above sea level.

Jellyfish can evaporate, remember.

Some scientists contend that all tigers originated, not in the tropics, but in the bleak cold of northern Asia.

Don't know how much 16 million tons (14.4 million tonnes) are, but do know that's how much rain and snow falls on the entire surface of the earth every second, average.

On this world, four-fifths of everything alive is in the sea, I'm told.

A chef reports it's possible to serve a different kind of fish every day for almost six months without repeating a single fish dish. Incredible!

Q. Who said, "Everybody talks about the weather, but nobody does anything about it"? Mark Twain or Will Rogers?

A. Both said it, but Charley Dudley Warner said it first.

7 Deranged Writers

Understand the library at England's Cambridge University has one shelf of books exclusively devoted to the works of deranged writers. That's right, only one shelf.

MALAPROPISMS

Takes a certain kind of mind to come up with a tasty malapropism, that sort of phrase wherein the wrong word is used with whimsy. Pat French of Great Falls, Montana, has such a mind. Some of her malaprop concoctions: "Indoor-outdoor carport . . . skinny dripping . . . extrasensory conception . . . inglowing toenails . . . Samson and Jemima . . . ravenous beauty . . . Saudi Uranium . . . Federal Bureau of Instigation . . . contract lenses . . . flowering inferno . . . confound interest." And to identify the carnival huckster who peddles ice cones: "the abdominal snowman."

Writing free verse is like playing tennis with the net down.
Robert Frost

Q. Which was invented first, the typewriter or the fountain pen?

A. The typewriter.

What, you can't identify which U.S. president wrote 37 books? The most prolific of the presidential authors, Teddy Roosevelt.

Q. Any truth to the old story that George Washington cut down his father's cherry tree, then confessed, saying "I cannot tell a lie?"

A. Not likely. A biographer named Parson Weems dreamed up that one. He put a lot of fiction in books about Benjamin Franklin and William Penn, too.

RUSSIAN ROULETTE

Who was the first poor soul to play that deadly game called Russian roulette? Name of that fellow is not at hand, but he wasn't a Russian, know that much. The English poet Lord Byron recorded in his memoirs how his roommate at Cambridge around 1808 pointed a partially loaded revolver at his own head and pulled the trigger. It just went snap, not bang. A Russian writer named Lermontov in 1839 expanded the Byron bit into a short story called "The Fatalist." Thereafter, a sufficient number of experimenters died in such gambles with the odds to make the deadly game well known.

FLEMING'S BOND. Among the favorite books of Ian Fleming was one called "Birds of the West Indies" by James Bond. That's where Fleming got his name for the 007 character.

Q. Did the writer Ernest Hemingway ever say what he thought was the greatest American novel?

A. Mark Twain's "Huckleberry Finn" was his choice. "It's the best book we've had," he said. "All American writing comes from that. There was nothing before. There has been nothing as good since."

The foregoing brings to mind this week's favorite classified ad: "Help Wanted—Traveling companion for raft trip down the Mississippi. Contact Huckleberry Finn. Equal opportunity employer."

Q. What's the difference between a clown, a comedian and a humorist?

A. A clown wants you to laugh at what he does, a comedian at what he says, a humorist at what he thinks. That's my notion. Will Rogers believed otherwise. A humorist, remarked he, is the one who scratches his head before he talks.

TOLSTOY

That great Russian writer Leo Tolstoy invited several people to dinner. One woman among them said she knew he was a vegetarian, but she personally preferred meat, so she asked him if he would be kind enough to serve her chicken. When she turned up at the table, she found a live chicken tied to her chair. "My conscience forbids me to kill it," said Tolstoy, "so I'd be greatly obliged if you'd do it for me." No, that's all I know.

It's not there anymore, but the sign that used to hang in the San Antonio Carnegie Library read: "Only low talk allowed."

BIRTH OF PHILO VANCE

Willard Huntingdon Wright was bright. Too bright, his doctor thought. So in 1922, said doctor confined Willard in a lonely room inside a Paris clinic. Notion was to cure that patient of his melancholy, his addiction to sedatives, his extreme physical weakness. The doctor opined that Willard intellectualized himself through a hypochondria into a real illness. So he refused to let Willard do anything there in solitary except read detective stories. Shucks, said Willard, or words to that effect, I can write better stuff than this. He dreamed up a fellow named Philo Vance, one of the great storybook sleuths, and wrote his way back to good health under the pseudonym of S. S. Van Dine. Remember him?

What the writers of mystery fiction don't realize, evidently, is the best lip readers in the world can only understand about a fourth of what's said.

58

Quite high on the long list of good news and bad news stories bouncing around the boondocks these days is that report by the masochist to the sadist: "I have some good news and some bad news, and the good news is there's a lot of bad news."

Q. Wasn't it the songwriter who coined the phrase "makin' whoopee?"

A. No, contrary to popular belief, the late columnist Walter Winchell originated that one.

PARAGRAPHS. Turning personal, a client asks why I write so many short paragraphs instead of just a couple of long ones. Can only reply by quoting old Harry V. Wade: "Paragraphing is one of the lower forms of cunning, like a way with women." It was Wade, too, who said, "Gypsy Rose Lee, the strip-tease artist, arrived in Hollywood with 12 empty trunks."

Who was the first of the daily newspaper columnists? That poet of childhood Eugene Field generally is so credited. His "Sharps and Flats" column started in the *Chicago Daily News* in 1883.

CHESS PLAYERS. A study of the world's great chess players reveals that a relatively large proportion of same were known to be mentally ill and seriously so. But an even larger proportion were recognized as extraordinarily gifted in other unrelated professions.

Q. Why is a "free lance writer" so called?

A. That goes back to Sir Walter Scott. He described the mercenary soldiers who hired out to anybody as free lances.

FOR THE BLIND

The publishers of Braille books for blind children are including in some of their volumes slips of special paper impregnated with various scents. These take the place of illustrations. The reader can scratch that paper to release a fragrance keyed to the story. Odor of pine arises from a forest scene. Wood smoke accompanies a campfire description. When mention is made of the purchase of a new car, up jumps banana oil. Excellent.

Figure a Braille book will be about 30 times bigger than the same book printed in ink.

He was a poet who didn't know it was William Whewell. In his "Elementary Treatise on Mechanics," he simply meant it as prose when he wrote: "And so no force, however great, can stretch a cord, however fine, into a horizontal line which shall be absolutely straight." It's the best known example in the English language of unconscious but perfect rhyme.

REDUNDANCY

Was none other than James M. Hotchkiss, Jr., who said, "To commit suicide in Philadelphia is an act of redundancy." Mr. Hotchkiss collects redundancies. Like: "Brief moment," "congregate around," "enclosed within," "end result," "military bomber," "past history," "close proximity," "original source," "proceed ahead," "totally annihilate," and "stupid idiot."

Q. How come George Orwell titled his book "1984" instead of, say, "1983" or "1985?"

A. He wrote it in '48. He just switched the last two digits.

Neglected to mention among the world's best-selling books that little volume known as "The Truth That Leads to Eternal Life" put out by the Watchtower Bible and Tract Society, Inc. with 74 million.

Can you identify what's extraordinary about the following sentence? "Gateman sees name, garageman sees name tag."

It's a palindrome, reading the same backwards as forwards. Few collectors of palindromes list that one. Others none too common are: "Pa's a sap." "Was it a car or a cat I saw?" And this common household statement: "I roamed under it as a tired nude Maori."

Q. Quick, Louie, name that famous poet who wrote the verse called "If"?

A. Which poet? Besides Rudyard Kipling, John Masefield and Emily Dickinson likewise wrote verses so-titled.

Q. Lawrence of Arabia claimed he had read 40,000 books during his stay at Oxford. Is that possible?

A. In a word, no. The professional readers who put in eight hours a day in publishing houses don't even come close to that. After 20 years of reading six or seven hours daily, Van Wyck Brooks, for instance, said he still hadn't read as many as 6,000 books. Adolf Hitler was another phony in this regard. He contended he had read 7,000 military books. Bunk! And included in the fiction of Thomas Wolfe was his nonsense report that he had read 20,000 books.

MAD AS A HATTER

The word "mad" once meant "poisonous." And "atter" was the old Anglo-Saxon word for that snake we call an "adder." Point is, our phrase "mad as a hatter" was not originally synonymous with "crazy," but meant "poisonous as an adder." Or so reports one authority. Interesting, if true. Our Language man long has been under the impression that "mad as a hatter" alluded to those numerous hatters who suffered mercury poisoning, an ailment common in that trade because of the use of quicksilver. A patient with mercury poisoning is apt to tremble uncontrollably, then get disoriented.

Another distinction merited by Mark Twain's great novel "Tom Sawyer" is the fact it was the first typed manuscript ever submitted to a publisher by an American author. In 1875, that was.

Q. What's the difference between a humorist and satirist?

A. Can only quote Father Ronald A. Knox on that one. Said he: "The humorist runs with the hare; the satirist hunts with the hounds."

To that list of famous men who started out as newsboys, please add Arthur Godfrey, Bing Crosby, Joe DiMaggio, John L. Lewis, Harry S. Truman, Frank Sinatra, Red Skelton, Bob Hope and General Omar Bradley.

BE BRIEF

Where I apprenticed in this dandy trade, the best of the newsmen wrote the tightest crispest copy. Once turned in a story, containing the sentence, "Raise it up a little higher." The city editor said, "Son, here's why I'm your boss." He struck out the word "higher." The managing editor, looking over his shoulder, said to him, "Mister, here's why I'm your boss." He struck out the words "up a little."

Note it stated in print that the word "earmarked" grew out of that frowned-upon practice of turning down the corner of a book page to show where the reading left off. That's not right. British farmers of old notched the ears of their cattle to identify them. That's the origin.

What children's books do you remember best from your youthful days? Surveytakers put that query to numerous famous Americans. They listed these: 1) Grimm's Fairy Tales, 2) Louisa May Alcott's works, 3) Alice in Wonderland, 4) The stories of Horatio Alger, Jr., 5) Mark Twain's writings, 6) Black Beauty, 7) Treasure Island, 8) Winnie the Pooh, and 9) The Bible.

Q. Didn't Dorothy Parker write "Excuse My Dust" as her own epitaph?

A. She wrote two. The other was: "Involved in a Plot."

Nowhere in print was there any reference to that game known as table tennis more than 94 years ago.

To his list of redundancies, our Language man now has added "daily journal."

That common compliment least appreciated by actors and artists and authors and such is said to be: "Keep up the good work."

GALSWORTHY. It's said of that great writer John Galsworthy that he much wanted a quiet place to work so he could complete his play called "Justice." The record shows he put on his oldest clothes, tossed a brick through a plate glass store front, and finished the manuscript during his next six months in jail.

No aspiring author should forget that it took Stephen Crane only 10 days to write that great tale "The Red Badge of Courage."

IT'S NOT TOO LATE

And no Seasoned Citizen should forget: Immanuel Kant wrote his best philosophical works at age 74. Verdi turned out "Ave Maria" at age 85. Goethe finished "Faust" at age 80. Tennyson did "Crossing the Bar" at age 80. Michelangelo completed his greatest art work at age 87. Titian painted the "Battle of Lepanto" at age 98. And Justice Oliver Wendell Holmes set down some of his most brilliant opinions at age 90.

FORTUNE COOKIES

Q. When do the Chinese fortune cookie makers put that little slip of paper into the cookie, before it's baked or after?

A. After. The cookie is baked flat. The slip of paper is put in the middle while it's still warm. Then the cookie cooker twists it into shape by hand and it hardens as it cools off.

King of the Chinese fortune cookie business, I'm told, is David Jung, a Los Angeleño. Turns out six million a year. He is said to enjoy such lines as: "You are in your own way—please stand aside." Oh, you don't like that? Then write your own. Understand he buys about 500 a year. Intend to sell him my best one: "Avoid exotic foods."

IS THERE A DOCTOR IN THE HOUSE?

How many physicians can you name who turned into best-selling authors? Start with Somerset Maugham. Add A. J. Cronin. Plus Frank Slaughter, and, of course, Benjamin Spock. But the list is far lengthier than that. This comes to mind because a customer asks the age of Dr. Peter Mark Roget when he compiled his famous "Roget's Thesaurus." He was 73. By age 90, he had put it through 28 editions. As previously reported, Roget was the best-selling physician in all of literature.

8 Abracadabra

Am asked where the magic makers came up with the word "abracadabra." That was the name of a god once worshipped by the Syrians, says our Language man.

Q. How many so-called witches were burned at the stake in Salem, Mass.?

A. None. Quite a few were hanged thereabouts, though. Specifically, no white woman convicted of witchcraft was burned in the United States. But the record shows one black woman was burned alive in 1779 at Kaskaskia, Illinois. And a dozen other black slaves were burned alive in 1741 in New York City. The witchhunters in Europe did not so discriminate. They burned a whole bevy of convicted witches without regard to complexion.

COLD CURE. A Czech medical fellow named Dr. Yinder Urban contends in the *Prague Medical Tribune* that he has promptly cured hundreds of patients who suffer from the common cold. Says he merely immerses their forearms for 60 minutes in water heated from 104 to 113 degrees F. (40 to 45 degrees C.). Amazing, if true. Are you skeptical? Likewise.

That famous Indian rope trick originated in China, not in India. And stuntmen in Germany performed it 200 years before it caught on among the Indian tricksters.

PHONE. "Miss your loved ones? Call long distance." Perfectly reasonable the telephone company should slip that filler line of house copy into the Yellow Pages. Unfortunately, it showed up at the bottom of the listings for funeral directors and thus made a most peculiar impact.

Please record that date when you hear the first thunder of the year. An ancient superstition contends the first frost will come exactly six months thereafter.

The U.S. Navy never launches a new ship on any Friday or on any 13th.

HICCUPS

Writes Sandra Monette: "Doubt a spoonful of ordinary table sugar is the best cure for hiccups. I'm convinced the eating of an ordinary banana works better, always."

Writes a Tacoma client: "What's an even better cure for hiccups than a teaspoonful of sugar is this: Place a clean handkerchief over the top of a glass of water and drink the water through the handkerchief. It works, it works!"

Writes Berni Robinson: "Let's settle this hiccup-cure question. A teaspoonful of sugar, a shot of vinegar, water drunk through a clean handkerchief, just nonsense! What works every time is this: Drink a half a glass of any non-alcoholic liquid, but in small sips, continually swallowing, swallowing, swallowing, without pause. You can drink a gallon, but still hiccup, if you don't follow swallow directly upon swallow."

Maybe it's just coincidence, but lengthy studies of the weather records show there are more thunderstorms around the world on the second day after the full moon than at any other time.

Report out of Kuala Lumpur says a 100-year-old medicine man there recently got married for the 78th time. That has to be a record, what? His latest bride was age 42.

Q. I read where that great magician Blackstone was able to stop his pulse at will. How?

A. Nothing to it. Anybody can. You, too. By putting a wad of cloth two inches thick under your armpit, then pressing hard against it.

TIMING. Peculiar thing about seagulls. Their built-in sense of time is precise. I mean they can take inland trips, but then return to shore to feed at the exact hour when the tide is right.

What's known is that geese can precisely predict stormy skies 12 hours in advance. What's not known is how.

Nowhere but in Japan is the spilling of salt regarded as a sign of good luck.

COBWEBS. You can expect fair weather if you see cobwebs on the grass. Many is the Seasoned Citizen who believes that, even without remembering why it's true. You can't see those cobwebs unless dew forms. And what's needed to form dew is a cloudless atmosphere with no wind. In other words, fair weather.

Too few people realize that those shooting stars we see flash across the sky usually are no bigger than wheat grains. Most of them burn out about 70 miles (112 km) up.

It was shortly before Columbus discovered America that designers in England and France first drew the faces of the Queens and the Kings and the Jacks that appear virtually unchanged today on our playing cards. Ugly, aren't they?

Am now advised that a "blue moon" refers to the second full moon in any one month. Do you know how frequently a second full moon in any one month occurs? About every 32 months on the average, research reveals.

Q. Is it true that a hypnotist can't make a subject do something contrary to that person's moral convictions? I mean, for instance, like cause a girl to take off all her clothes in public?

A. On the contrary. Some fairly fascinating research back in 1947 proved that a hypnotist indeed could cause anti-social behavior. Just by convincing the subject that such behavior was necessary. If that girl, for example, were led to believe that she were alone in her bathroom and that her clothes were infested with biting ants, she might very well strip to the buff in front of an audience.

The record shows that even as far back as 3000 B.C. the Egyptians practiced that thing called hypnotism.

SNAKE CHARMERS

How can an Indian snake charmer charm a cobra by playing a flute in light of the widely known fact that said snake is deaf? Pretty tricky. A snake like that will strike at the nearest warm or moving object. And it will only strike a prescribed distance in proportion to the length of its body, depending on the container it's rising out of. To make the snake sit up and look around, the charmer taps on the ground to send vibrations. To make the snake weave and bob, the charmer himself weaves and bobs, now a little closer and now a little farther away. If the charmer were to make the mistake of getting too close, the snake would strike the end of the flute. That's what the flute is for. To protect the charmer's hands and face.

Among those betting citizens who play the lottery, it's a common superstition that the odd numbers are more likely to win than the even.

Statistics indicate arsonists set more fires during the full moon than at any other time.

CANDLE. If a candle's flame turns blue, there's a ghost in the house. If a candle sends out a spark, the party nearest that spark can expect a letter soon. If a candle is hard to light, wet weather is predicted. The foregoing are items Nos. 7, 8 and 9-C in our Old Superstitions file.

Q. Over the years, which has sold better, the Monopoly set or the ouija board?

A. The ouija board. It's older.

LUCKY NUMBER. Do you have a lucky number? Among those people in the U.S.A. who say yes to that query, the majority designate 7 as said number. Worldwide, however, the number 9 is considered the luckiest by the most people.

DICE

Some men of science have gone so far as to try to prove that you can influence the roll of dice by talking to them. When they rolled the dice 100 times in silence, seven came up 16 times. When they rolled 100 times while repeating "come on seven," that seven came up 19 times. They tried the experiment repeatedly. And always got more sevens when they chanted to the dice. They're now convinced. More convinced than I, might mention.

Tough skin on the apples is said to foretell a severe winter, reports our Old Superstitions man.

Stargazers insist that the Sagittarian tends to have a green thumb.

Many a woman and man these days claims to be a witch. Did you know the origin of the word "witch?" Came from the Anglo-Saxon *wica* meaning "wise one."

To his collection of palindromes, phrases that spell the same backwards as forwards, our Language man has added one line from a conversation about how to cure warts: "Straw, no, too stupid a fad, I put soot on warts."

Four out of five gypsies travel very little, if at all.

TRICK

Write down the numbers 1, 2, 3, 4, 5, 6, 7, 9. Notice, please, there's no 8. Now which of those numerals was hardest to write. You say the 7? All right, multiply the entire 12345679 by 63. Correct, your answer will consist only of 7s. Doesn't matter which number you say is hardest to write. Trick here is the multiplying is done by nine times that number, whatever it is. So if you select 9, then you would multiply by 81. If you select 2, then multiply by 18. So on.

Actor David Niven wore the same old trench coat in at least one scene of every movie he made. His own personal garment, not from wardrobe. A foible for luck.

Try this color test on yourself. Your preferences may indicate something about your personality, according to recent studies. Intellectuals like blue. Athletes prefer red. Congenial party types pick orange. Egotists go for yellow. And the lovelorn, those unfortunate souls, develop a thing about purple.

What the editor inadvertently left out of the 1860 Farmer's Almanac was the weather prediction for July 13. But the typesetter, a whimsical fellow, decided "rain" and "snow" and "hail" would fill in the blank quite nicely. He figured the editor would correct the thing on the proof. The editor didn't. That typesetter must have had a direct connection. On July 13, it rained, snowed, hailed.

HOW TO LOAD DICE

Q. How is it possible to load transparent dice?

A. Nothing to it. Let them stand for a few weeks in a saucer containing mineral oil about an eighth of an inch deep. The impregnated side of each die thereafter will be a little heavier than the other sides, so will tend to wind up on the underside at each throw.

Q. Can you say that all the roulette wheels in Las Vegas are honest?

A. No, but certainly most are. Why should a house rig a wheel when it already has a minimum hedge of from 5 to 19 per cent against the player on every bet?

TRICKY MATH

What's your age? Don't tell me. Just multiply it by 3. Add 1. Multiply that by 3. Add your age again. Knock off the last digit. What do you get? Your age. But then you knew that.

9 Too Many Ink Spots

Since the breakup of those renowned harmonizers known as the original Ink Spots, more than 40 singing groups have used that name.

Q. Of those people photographed unawares by Allen Funt's "Candid Camera," how many refused to let their pictures be shown on television?

A. About three out of every 1,000, says Funt. And 75 per cent of those who refuse are men, he says.

Children aged 4 to 6 were surveyed on the question: "Which do you like better, TV or daddy?" Forty-four per cent said TV.

That singing Boone named Pat started out as Charles Eugene.

OPERA SINGERS. Can you explain why so many opera singers are greatly overweight? A Harvard psychiatrist says it's because they give out with all that music, so feel they must take in with all that food. They sense that they're owed something orally. Maybe so, don't know.

So you want to be a radio announcer, young fellow? All right, say, "The clothes moths' mouths closed on red leather, yellow leather." Not bad. Now say it again faster.

CHORUS LINE. You've seen those high kicks of the modern chorus line? Nothing new, that routine. A relief carving that dates back to 2500 B.C. in Egypt depicts exactly the same. A long chain of Egyptian chorines decked out in transparent costumes are shown with their legs thrown high in that precision kick.

Q. Julie Andrews, is that her real name?

A. She started out as Julia Wells.

OLD FAVORITES

So you think songs come and go so fast that nobody remembers them for long, do you? Maybe lately. But these were the most popular six tunes at exactly the turn of the century: "In the Shade of the Old Apple Tree," "In the Good Old Summertime," "Sweet Adeline," "Meet Me in St. Louis," "Mighty Lak' a Rose" and "Wait Till the Sun Shines Nellie." Can't you still hum each of them? Likewise.

Q. Has Nancy Sinatra had a nose job?

A. She has said so.

ACTRESS. Name the famous lady who said, "I don't care what you do, my dear, so long as you don't do it in the street and frighten the horses." That was Mrs. Patrick Campbell, the great actress. She was one of the few renowned entertainers, incidentally, who always insisted she be billed on marquees with the Mrs. and her husband's name. Can you think of any others who did likewise?

That word "ventriloquism" comes from some Latin syllables which translate roughly as "stomach talk."

Tap the lowest key on your piano, if any. Am told the sound can't be heard by your dog, if any. Try it.

"GOD MOVES"

That dandy hymn "God Moves in a Mysterious Way His Wonders to Perform" was composed in 1799 by William Cowper of London. That's widely known. Less widely known is what caused him to write it. One evening he became so melancholy he decided to commit suicide. He hailed a taxicab and told the driver to take him to a Thames River bridge. But the fog was thick. After an hour of wandering aimlessly, the cab man said he gave up, he couldn't find the bloomin' bridge, and he didn't even know how to get his fare back home. Cowper stepped out only to realize he was right in front of his own room. That's when he went indoors to write "God Moves . . ."

Q. Can an ostrich sing?

A. Singing is no name for it, definitely not. However, its various call notes outnumber those of most songbirds.

TAP DANCING. High-speed recordings indicate no tap dancer ever beats out more than 840 taps per minute.

Q. What name did actor Mike Connors start out with?

A. Krekor Ohanian.

You know what an obbligato is—a song that can be played simultaneously with another song. "Dinah" and "Stardust" duet like that. Such pairs of songs are not so unusual. But to the foregoing two, you can also add "By the Waters of Minnetonka" to make a trio. The three largest orchestras in the country could play these songs together, one each, and you wouldn't hear a dischord.

Q. You know that theme song of "All in the Family?" It's called "Those Were the Days." Nobody around here can get the next to the last line.

A. It goes: "Gee, our old LaSalle ran great."

History records the fact the New York State Assembly passed resolutions at one time or another to ban the tango, the rhumba, the mambo and the cha cha.

TELEVISION

So you thought the United States was tops in television, did you? No, there are 401 TV sets for every 1,000 Swedes, only 399 for every 1,000 U.S. citizens. Man for man, the Swedes read more newspapers, too, incidentally.

No average citizen worldwide watches more television per week than the Japanese, I'm told.

Did you know a cat is more inclined to watch television than is a dog? So say the animal experts. Compared to a dog, a cat relies more on its vision, less on its sense of smell, that's why.

Q. Is Mike Douglas his real name?

A. No. He started out as Michael Delaney Dowd Jr.

FEARS

It's widely known that the two most basic human fears are the fear of falling and the fear of loud noises. Highwire performers with circuses long have relied on the falling fear to fascinate audiences. But sometime back, a particularly clever tightrope walker decided to take advantage of the other fear, too. Throughout his act, he screamed and bellowed, then climaxed the bit by touching off a string of firecrackers as he faked a fall. Was too much. The performance shook up the onlookers so badly it wasn't repeated.

It was NBC-TV that started a six-week course for stuntmen which included a class in "Elementary Street Brawling."

Was at least 20 years after he wrote "Take Me Out to the Ball Game" that Albert von Tilzer saw his first baseball game.

People who don't know much about music tend to hear it better in the left ear than in the right. But musicians seem to hear it better in the right ear than in the left. The why of this peculiarity I can't explain, sorry to say. It was reported by a pair of Columbia University scholars who made an extensive study of the matter.

COMMERCIALS. If you wonder why you see the same commercials repeatedly, consider this: Approximately 22 per cent of the TV ad money is paid out by only 10 big sponsors.

That outfit known as the Marketing Science Institute reports that hardly any children over 10 years old believe the ads on TV.

This week's favorite classified ad reads: "Sparky's Appliance Shop: Reduction on TV Sets! All 19-inch sets have been reduced to 12 inches."

WANT TO BUY A DUCK?

Consider yourself a Seasoned Citizen, if you remember the burlesque comic Joe Penner, whose routine almost invariably included the query: "Want to buy a duck?" Why was that line funny? Most mysterious. Yet it brought the house down every time. Penner himself never understood it. In building his act, he originally asked: "Want to buy a horse?" Then: "Want to buy an elephant?" And: "Want to buy a giraffe?" Nobody laughed. But the audience always roared over the "duck" line.

GARGLE. The television code of the National Association of Broadcasters forbids any scene wherein somebody gargles. I'm glad.

Am frequently asked the difference between a fiddle and a violin. All experts consulted in this matter, except one, say there's no difference, really. The exception, Mr. Loid Tennison, contends you carry a violin in a case, a fiddle in a flour sack, that's all.

CAT-IN-THE-BOX

What was the name of the first theatrical director to use the famous cat-in-the-box trick? That was the remarkable piece of stage business wherein a cat crawled out from under a chair on cue to stretch itself in front of a fireplace. David Belasco was the genius. On Nov. 17, 1879, he opened the play entitled "Hearts of Oak" in Hamlin's Theater in Chicago. Every night when the curtain went up, out crawled the feline to stretch. Nothing to it. An hour earlier, Belasco crammed that cat into a small box, then pulled open its trap door with a wire offstage. You bet that cramped animal stretched when loose. Who wouldn't?

May I suggest that Telly Savalas, Yul Brynner and the like stay out of that nation called Chile? Was customary there for a long time to make pickpockets easily identifiable by shaving their heads.

So up jumps Allen Funt with his Candid Camera show again. Excellent. Do you know how he first got that notion? During World War II, he was put on a project to develop concealment techniques. He not only learned how to hide men and arms, but cameras and microphones, too. At war's end, he converted his technical savvy to that appealing Candid Camera game.

SPINOFFS

In 1952, June Allyson and Humphrey Bogart starred in a film called "Battle Circus," wherein was shown a Mobile Army Surgical Hospital, actually a "M*A*S*H" unit. Now may I make a point? Most of the best shows are spinoffs. Only rarely does an Orson Welles or a Woody Allen come up with a compelling original.

Q. You know Jack Lord of "Hawaii Five-O?" Is that his real name?

A. He started out as J. J. Ryan. Incidentally, were you aware that he's an artist of some renown? Three of his woodcuts and two of his lithographs hang in the Metropolitan Museum of Art.

Was none other than Gene Fowler who said, "Success is a toy balloon among children armed with sharp pins."

10 Our Gang

Q. How many "Our Gang/Little Rascals" comedy films were produced in all?

A. Exactly 221.

Q. How many "Our Gang/Little Rascals" comedies did Robert "Baretta" Blake appear in?

A. Exactly 40 in five years.

What's your favorite movie of all time? Adolf Hitler's was "King Kong."

Q. How did Alfred Hitchcock, who always showed up for a moment in each film he directed, manage to do that thing in "Lifeboat" where the whole show took place in a small boat with only a few well-defined characters?

A. In the bottom of the boat was a newspaper. Somebody turned it over. On the back page was a before-and-after weight-reducing advertisement. Hitchcock was the before.

It's a matter of record, too, that Sophia Loren's husband, Carlo Ponti, gave his wife for her fortieth birthday a 14-carat gold toilet seat. Correspondents say it was custom fitted, but they won't say how.

Actor Charles Bronson reports that his family was so poor he started school in dresses outgrown by his sister.

You already knew that Rock Hudson's real name was Roy Scherer, didn't you?

CASTING

If the original Hollywood planners had had their way, Edward G. Robinson would have starred in "The Petrified Forest." Ronald Reagan, in "Casablanca." George Raft, in "The Maltese Falcon." And Gregory Peck, in "The African Queen." Details that explain how Humphrey Bogart wound up as the star in each of the foregoing films are lengthy and complicated. But he did, in fact. More recently, the late Mr. Bogart turned into a sort of cult worshipers' hero. But the old pros in Hollywood say he almost never was the first choice of the casting moguls. That's hard to understand, isn't it?

WESTERN

Q. Who starred in the first western movie?

A. Buffalo Bill Cody. And it was Thomas Edison who ran the camera, incidentally. In New Jersey.

That classic actress Greta Garbo has never given anybody her autograph, I'm told.

Q. How did actor Glenn Ford get into show business?

A. His first such job was manager of a burlesque house in San Francisco.

Q. What's Yul Brynner's real name?

A. Alfie Jones, notes the record at hand.

Which came first, color movies or sound movies? Wait, don't be too swift. First color film was "Toll of the Sea" in 1922.

First full length sound film was "The Jazz Singer" in 1927. You can win bets with this question.

This notion has been traditional among the movie makers: That almost any girl looks good coming down stairs. And almost none looks good going up. Exceptions? None, they say.

Q. What was the first Hollywood movie for general public release to use dirty words?

A. "Who's Afraid of Virginia Woolf."

SPEED. Most widely recognized signal words on a movie set are "lights," "camera," "action." But there is a fourth signal word less known. It's "speed." That's what the audio recorder calls out to tell the director that the camera is revved up enough to accept the sound without distortion.

WHAT DO YOU WANT TO SEE TONIGHT?

Movies used to be made mostly for women. On the theory a fellow always asked his girl, "What do you want to see tonight?" Movies now, however, are made for young men. On the theory the lad of the new ilk no longer asks, just takes her. Such is the serious claim of a Hollywood expert. "No joke," he insists, "box office proves it. The boys pick the shows now. The girls just go along for the kicks."

Television came on the scene fairly strongly in 1948. That year the American moviemakers turned out 448 films. In 1958 the moviemakers produced 352. In 1968 they only brought forth 258. And in 1977 they made 186. This gives you some notion about what TV has done to the motion picture business.

MOST CLOTHES

Am asked what Hollywood actor of all time has been the most clothes conscious. Cesar Romero, possibly. According to the most recent report at hand, his wardrobe count: 500 suits, 190 sports jackets and 30 tuxedos.

Who remembers Douglas Fairbanks, Sr.? For that matter, who remembers Douglas Fairbanks, Jr.? Anyhow, Douglas, Sr., in his heyday, owned 454 suits, one for every day of the year plus two for each Sunday and holiday.

WESTERNS. Do you know what proportion of the movies made in the U.S.A. have been westerns? A third of them. And that goes all the way back to the first movie called "The Kiss." Westerns still are the most popular shows on TV. Then come the action adventure plays. Next the mystery suspense programs. And after that, the comedies.

Q. Is it true that actor Clint Walker is a vegetarian?

A. So go the reports. Likewise Dennis Weaver and Paul Newman.

Q. How old is Donald Duck?

A. He was born in 1934.

That great actor Spencer Tracy once mistakenly was given an Academy Award engraved Dick Tracy.

You might find useful this handy movie guide from Elston Brooks: "If the picture is rated 'G,' the hero gets the girl. If it's rated 'R,' the villain gets her. If it's rated 'X,' everybody gets her."

No motion picture made in Japan before World War II was permitted by censors there to have any kissing scenes.

INDIAN FILMS. How many motion pictures have you seen that were made by East Indians in India? Not many, if any, I'll warrant. So it's noteworthy, is it not, that India has the third largest motion picture industry in the world? Right behind Japan and the United States.

Q. What did that old cowboy actor Tom Mix do before he became a movie star?

A. He was a U.S. marshal, sir.

GONE WITH THE WIND

Consider the cast of major actors and actresses in that classic film "Gone With the Wind." Am asked who among them, if any, survive today? Only Olivia DeHaviland. Gone are Clark Gable, Vivian Leigh, Leslie Howard, Laura Hope Crews, Paul Hurst, Harry Davenport, Ward Bond, Hattie McDaniel, George Reeves, Olin Howland. Gone also, writer Margaret Mitchell, scenarist Sidney Howard, director Victor Fleming, designer William Menzies. Here's to them all—clink! And to Miss DeHaviland, too, the pretty lady.

Q. What's actor Charles Bronson's real name?

A. Charles Buchinsky.

CAINE. Was from a movie marquee displaying "The Caine Mutiny Court-Martial" that actor Michael Caine got his stage surname. Believe you already know he started out as Maurice Joseph Micklewhite.

Who remembers Lana Turner? Numerous fraternity brothers, certainly. In her sweater-girl days, she was named the sweetheart of 38 different college fraternities. No other actress before or since has been so honored.

Q. The late Clark Gable was billed as "The King of Hollywood," but who was "The Queen?"

A. Myrna Loy. They got the labels as a result of a radio contest by Ed Sullivan in 1938. The nickname stuck with Gable somehow, but not quite with Miss Loy.

The great W. C. Fields kept his library in his bathroom.

Q. I've heard Dean Martin got his nose reshaped without any anesthetic whatsoever, right?

A. The first time. When he got it bent. The second time he had anesthetic. When he got it fixed.

Q. What's the name of the shark in "Jaws?"

A. The filming crew called it Bruce. Incidentally, it wasn't just one shark, but three. A right-sided shark with its instruments on the left. A left-sided shark with its instruments on the right. And a whole shark the crewmen called the floater.

COWBOYS AND HORSES. Not everybody has forgotten the names of the screen cowboys and their horses. A customer matches some of them up this way: Buck Jones, Silver Buck, called Silver B; Hoot Gibson, Whitey; Ken Maynard, Tarzan; William S. Hart, Fritz; Tex Ritter, White Flash.

ACTORS

You knew that actor David Niven used to lumberjack in Canada, didn't you? That James Caan got his start by carrying quarters of beef around a meat market? That Sebastian Cabot once chauffeured a London limousine? That Clint Eastwood never spent more than one semester in the same school? That Glenn Ford was born Gwyllen Ford, but eventually named himself after his father's Canadian birthplace, a little Quebec town called Glenford?

COCONUT. Ever recall seeing Bing Crosby and Dorothy Lamour romancing at night under a coconut tree? That wouldn't have happened if they'd been wise natives. The stems of mature coconuts become unsealed only at night. Has to do with the dew. Except in storms, coconuts rarely fall in the daytime. But any couple who knows their coconuts will get out from under that tree after dark.

In 1929, one John Grierson made a two-reel film about the British herring fleet. He called it "Drifters." And he coined a word to identify its type: documentary.

VOICE. What the voice of the prehistoric Tyrannosaurus really sounded like nobody knows. But in the movie "Dinosaurus," it sounded like the scratch of sandpaper plus the roar of a jet engine plus the crying of a baby, because that is what it was.

Actor Walter Matthau was 6 feet tall at age 11. It was about that time, he says, when he beat up a neighborhood kid named Rocky Graziano.

"Stagecoach" was the movie that made John Wayne a star. But the late Gary Cooper was the first choice for that role. The film "High Noon" revitalized Cooper's career. But Wayne was the original selection for that role.

KING KONG

Am asked how that great ape King Kong was made to move on the screen in the original 1933 classic. Stop motion animation is what that film technique is called. The camera boys shoot one frame at a time, manually changing the position of the big beast between each exposure. Slow process. Requires about three days that way to get 15 seconds of running film.

Shirley Maclaine says she was named after Shirley Temple.

Am asked to name the first film ever to gross over $1 million dollars. "Tarzan of the Apes," it was. Starred the first Tarzan, Elmo Lincoln.

Edgar Rice Burroughs' "Tarzan" books have been made into 38 motion pictures and 52 TV shows. Maybe you've heard that Burroughs never went to Africa.

The original voice of Mickey Mouse during his first 20 years was none other than that of Walt Disney himself.

Q. Is it true that Judy Garland was the lowest paid star in that film classic "The Wizard of Oz?"

A. Almost true. Only the dog Toto earned less.

11

There Must Be a Better Way

BACON. A Los Angeles librarian reports she finally found it necessary to pick up a gentleman's library card. Because her letters to him, telephone calls, and face-to-face pleas still failed to break him of the peculiar habit of using strips of raw bacon as bookmarks.

The U.S. Postal Service sent out a big batch of pamphlets that told citizens how to wrap Christmas parcels for mailing. But in Des Moines, Iowa, the package containing those pamphlets accidentally broke open, scattering them all over the place.

FILE IT. Did I ever tell you that less than 1 per cent of the paperwork filed away in your office is ever seen again by anybody three days after it's filed? And less than 5 per cent is ever seen again at all?

In South Africa, two farmers have trained a pair of ostriches to herd sheep. Those birds unattended take the woolies out in the morning and bring them back at night. But if a sheep dies, neither fowl nor flock shows up. The birds continue to peck at the dead carcass in an effort to drive it home. Fifteen minutes late means the farmers have to go out and they know why.

JEANS. In Southern California, many a ladies' wear boutique equips its dressing room with a cot-size mattress. The girls who shop for jeans and slacks like that. It permits them to lie down for try-ons so they can zip up to get that skin-tight fit.

ADVERTISING. If all the money spent on advertising every year were billed to the citizenry, U.S. residents would pay something in the neighborhood of $90 each. Predictably, the United States is where the most ad action is, worldwide. Nepal is where the least is. There, the total ad bill breaks down to 5 cents per resident.

A store in San Angelo, Texas, was burglarized sometime back. Friends advised the owner to lock up a couple of watch dogs in his place at night. He decided against that. Instead, just before he closes shop now, he turns loose inside a batch of rattlesnakes. A "Beware" sign on the front door reports the situation. He cages them again every morning.

Here's a claim that's hard to swallow. Most of what you and I do every day is routine, says a San Francisco scholar. Correct, so far. Driving, eating, washing, typing, shaving, walking, whatnot. In fact, the average man, he insists studies show, only devotes 60 seconds out of every hour in vigilant concentration to the work at hand. That's the claim that's curious, I think. If true, you and I spend only about 16 minutes every day paying attention.

PLACEBOS. You've heard of that innocuous sugar pill known as the "placebo," but did you know that in Latin it means "I will please"? Studies at Cornell University indicate the placebo pill seems to do its job better if it's either pink or blue. And it works even more spectacularly, if it's mottled.

DOUBLE BED

The standard double bed for grownups is only twice as wide as the standard crib for infants. Ridiculous! For sound uninterrupted sleep, a double bed with two occupants should be 22 inches (55 cm) wider than it is. This is not just one more of our Love and War man's whimsical theories. It comes from an authority who has made an extensive study of sleep, beds and widths of horizontal people.

The Japanese have come out with a vending machine that freshly cooks and serves spaghetti with meat sauce in 27 seconds. Ach!

One out of every four college students winds up in a job that doesn't require such a degree.

CHILD PSYCHOLOGY

The record shows that a New York City mother paid the going rate—is it $50 an hour?—to a psychoanalyst three times a week to read comic books to her 6-year-old son. This went on for quite a while. She was tempted to discontinue the treatment, she subsequently reported, but the doctor urged her not to stop, saying he needed more time to find out why the boy wanted him to read to him that way.

COLDS. If you have no youngsters in the house, odds run four to one that you'll get a cold this year. Odds go higher with children thereabouts.

Average person is said to get 140 colds in a lifetime.

DEODORANTS. The Bedouins of the Negev and Sinai deserts wear homemade deodorants. Clove buds strung together like beads, soaked in water, then worn around the neck. As they dry, they deodorize. Wait, that's not quite right. Rather they overcome all aromas but their own. Bedouins as a rule smell fairly clovey.

Was Cathy Carlyle who described love as an electric blanket with somebody else in control of the switch.

89

SPIDERS. If you've seen a house spider stomping around your place each of the last three days, you might as well hang in there patiently for another 24 hours. Normal longevity of those miniscule animals is only four days.

There was a time when men about to go to bed strapped cardboard boxes over their chins to keep their beards from getting tangled up while they slept.

Q. If you were to barbecue an elephant, what part would be the tastiest?

A. The footpads, I'm told.

PERFUME

Those professional perfume sniffers called "noses" work in sound-proof rooms, if possible, because noise dulls the sense of smell.

The ladies of old Rome customarily put perfumed swan's fat in their bathtubs filled with donkey milk.

Fascinating, the notations some doctors write on death certificates. The Missouri Board of Health recently turned up these: 1. "Death induced by blow on head with ax. Contributory cause—another man's wife." 2. "Went to bed feeling fine, but woke up feeling dead." 3. "Died suddenly. Nothing serious."

Can think of no tax in history more ridiculous than the "teeth money" tax levied in Turkey 250 years ago. When a pasha visited a peasant family, he customarily ate a free meal. Afterwards, he collected a tax to compensate him for the wear on his teeth.

Officials in the French government in the days of Voltaire set up a national lottery. But they weren't much good at math. They miscalculated. Voltaire, however, was indeed good at math. He put together a syndicate and bought up every ticket. His take of the winnings made him financially independent. It was only then he found time to write. Remember that, young fellow. If you want to be a writer, do your arithmetic.

Am acquainted with a couple of dairy hands who won't believe this, but in Texas it's against the law for any person to milk anybody else's cow.

A youngster is likely to be damaged psychologically if orphaned, or if an only child, or if the youngest, or if in the middle, or if the oldest. That's what I've learned of late from numerous studies of the matter. There's only one way to escape this damage. Be born grownup.

Pirates were not generally despised but rather greatly admired by most of the people in old England. Courts there had trouble finding juries that would convict them. Why so? Those buccaneers sold so much stolen stuff at such low prices that they came to be regarded as public benefactors.

EXCUSES. City editors are a cynical lot. Years ago, when H. Allen Smith was a reporter, he telephoned the office to say he couldn't get to work that day because he had slipped on the ice. Replied his city editor: "How did you get your foot in the glass?"

What, you didn't know some kangaroos live in treetops?

All grownups at one time or another in their lives have had mononucleosis. Or so the medics believe. That, they say, is why it rarely afflicts anybody over 30. Immunity sets in early. Once you've had it, you'll never get it again.

THE FIRST SHAGGY DOG STORY

A literary-minded client says he has come up with what he seriously believes to be the first of all the shaggy dog stories.

91

Considerably edited, it goes: In the days of the knights, a midget told his king that he, too, wanted to be a knight. Too small, said the king. But the determined midget went about the kingdom, catching highwaymen and rescuing maidens, until the news got back to the king. "All right," said the king, "I dub thee knight." Special miniature armor was hammered out for him. A galley knife was honed into a sword. But no horse little enough was found. So the king substituted a large shaggy dog. And the midget went forth again to do good. A terrible rainstorm came up. He rode to a nearby inn. But the innkeeper said there was no more room. The midget pointed out how little space he'd take up. The innkeeper looked him over, and his mount, too, both soaked to the skin, and finally said, "Come on in. We'll find a spot for you. I couldn't send a knight out on a dog like this."

The U.S. Department of Agriculture spent $113,417 to find out that mothers generally prefer children's clothing that needs no ironing. You could have told the Department that for half the price, what?

A medical specialist who has done considerable research in the back country of the Philippines contends that people who habitually sit on the ground instead of in chairs do not develop that ailment known as varicose veins.

Now standing where once stood that Philadelphia house in which Thomas Jefferson wrote the Declaration of Independence is a take-out hamburger joint.

Drowning victims when found are always face down.

Robert Chesebrough, the fellow who concocted that petroleum jelly known as Vaseline®, lived to age 96. And do you know to what he credited his longevity? The fact that he swallowed a spoonful of Vaseline® every day of his life after age 22, when he put the first batch of the stuff together.

It's said no squirrel ever remembers where he buried that nut.

TAILS. A man of medicine claims surgery at the base of the spinal cord has been known to cure convulsions, migraine headaches and neuralgia. He believes said surgery relieves tension which may cause such. That's interesting. But not as interesting, I think, as his additional contention that those animals which wag their tails do not suffer from convulsions, migraine headaches and neuralgia. And that human beings would not be so afflicted if they had tails to wag.

If you've ever thrown pine cones into a campfire, you may recall how the heat explodes them. Or almost. Anyhow, it opens them up in a hurry, releasing their seeds. That's why little pine trees spring up so quickly on those black lands burned over by forest fires. The fire plants the new forest immediately. This is Item No. 1472C in our Ain't Nature Wonderful file.

It's a matter of historical record that Dr. Sigmund Freud, the world's foremost authority in his day on sex, voluntarily put an end to his own indulgences in physical romance at about the age of 40.

Things that never come out even: Envelopes and stationery. Spaghetti and sauce. Pencil and eraser. Hotdogs and rolls. Stamps and valentines. What else? A hole and its refill dirt.

What do you eat for breakfast? When did you finish your Christmas shopping last year? How many unfilled dental cavities do you have? Don't answer, too personal. But these three queries are significant, according to a lady who hires the help for a big company. Her theory is people who eat good breakfasts, Christmas shop early, and get their teeth filled promptly make the most efficient workers.

Say the average working man puts in an eight-hour day. His earnings for one hour three minutes of that time go to pay for his housing. One hour two minutes makes him enough money to buy his food and beverages. Exactly 40 minutes supports the cost of his transportation. He needs to work 26 minutes to buy his clothing. Medical expenses require 23 minutes. He can figure 19 minutes for recreation. And his taxes will call for two hours 34 minutes of his day's labor. As for the rest, label it "other."

HEALTH

Some medicos contend that one out of every ten people nationwide are sick, but sick only because they think they're sick. In other words, hypochondriacs. That's not one out of ten who are sick, but one out of ten, counting everybody.

It's commonly believed that personal misfortunes lead to serious illness. If you lose your life savings and your mortgage is foreclosed and your mate runs off with a lover, you can expect next to be hit in the health. Happens too frequently to be coincidental, say the science boys. Less widely known is the fact that the reverse is true, too. If you suddenly come into a lot of money and find yourself appointed as the chairman of the board and surprisingly fall into a perfect romance, you again may expect serious illness. Such were the findings of an extensive study at the University of Washington's School of Medicine. To edit down the 114-page dissertation on the matter. It sure is weird.

Eighty per cent of the car wrecks wherein people get hurt happen on clear days.

TAKE A BATH. Was a time in Paris where baths were sold door-to-door. No, not bathtubs. Baths. More than 1,000 vendors drove carts with large tubs of hot water through the streets. They sang out. And citizens in need hailed them down.

Middle age, it's said, is that time of life when you're pushed around by two little voices, one saying, "Why not?" and the other saying, "Why bother?" Sound about right?

SNEAKY DOCTOR. Pretty cagey, this old doctor. Built a regional reputation for invariably predicting correctly the sex of an unborn infant. Upon his retirement, he explained. Aloud, he declared it would be a boy, but in his notebook he wrote the word "girl." If boy turned out to be right, he just smiled. But if the baby proved to be a girl, he whipped out his notebook to show the folks they must have heard him wrong. Sneaky. Very sneaky.

The most successful of men are frequently those who suffered the most miserable of childhoods. So says a scholar who has made a study of the matter. It is the only compensation that occurs to him, he says, for getting kicked around overmuch as a youngster. "Resentment breeds resourcefulness and anger breeds ambition," he says, sagely.

Studies indicate that about 50 per cent of the medicine prescribed by doctors is never taken by the patients.

GARLIC. I can't verify the claim, but some scholars at the University of California's Riverside Division of Biological

Control contend people who eat a lot of garlic aren't bitten by mosquitoes much, if at all.

PEARLS. Was the Japanese, as you might expect, who taught the Northern Australians how to induce oysters to grow pearls. Now those Australian experts are turning out marble-sized pearls in half the time it takes the Japanese to do likewise. Whatever their secret is, they're not publishing it.

There are two times in a man's life when he should not speculate: when he can't afford it, and when he can.

Mark Twain

That gambling debts are legally uncollectible is common knowledge. With this in mind, a client wants to know how much money the big Las Vegas casinos lose every year on welshers. About $8 million is the official estimate. The old pros thereabouts guess double that.

It was no more than 63 years ago that U.S. Secretary of State Philander Knox rarely returned to his office after lunch, saying, "There's just not enough work to do to occupy the Secretary's entire day."

Dr. Paul Rankin of Ohio State University undertook to find out how much time the average person spends in communications. He concluded: About 9 per cent in writing, 16 per cent in reading, 30 per cent in speaking and 45 per cent in listening. When I told the Ladyfriend she could save 30 per cent of her time by not talking, she said, "Why bother? I already save 45 per cent by not listening."

12 The Fairest of Them All

Familiarity is a magician that is cruel to beauty, but kind to ugliness.

Ouida

At first glance, you wouldn't think the bird of paradise, one of the world's most beautiful feathered critters, was a kissing cousin of the crow, would you? It is.

GUM BALLS. You know those simple little machines that used to give you a gum ball for a penny? Their take doubled when some bright soul put mirrors on some of them. Customers who really wanted to see their reflections could do so less conspicuously if they dropped a cent into a slot at the same time.

Certainly no single girl should forget the immortal words of Clare Boothe Luce, as follows: "When a woman is alone, there are four things she must do. Dress like a girl, act like a lady, think like a man, and work like a horse."

BIKINIS

Nothing new about that swimsuit known as the bikini. Archaeologists dug up an old Roman villa sometime back. And found in the ruins some mosaic plaques which show Roman girls in some sort of frolic around a swimming pool. Quite right, in bikinis.

It is a matter of record, too, that in the year A.D. 400, the bathing beauties of Sicily wore bikinis.

Did I tell you it's illegal in Norfolk, Virginia, for a girl to go to a public dance unless she wears a corset?

BURNS. The death rate among women as a result of burns in the last 15 years has dropped by 55 per cent. Researchers studied and studied to find out why. But they reported they could turn up no other reason than the fact that far more women of late are wearing pantsuits and slacks instead of dresses and skirts.

That pantsuit color most frequently preferred by women with gray hair is some shade of pink.

Q. Isn't it a fact two thirds of all the long distance telephone calls are made by women?

A. From home phones only.

The average woman uses up approximately her height in lipstick every five years.

If you're under the impression that ladies in nudist camps tend to use more makeup than ladies elsewhere, you're right.

Do you realize approximately three million women in this country sport tattoos?

Wouldn't do to dwell overmuch here on mammary glands, don't suppose, but it is a medical fact that approximately one out of every 200 women has more than the customary number of same.

Q. Why do women's blouses button differently from men's shirts?

A. Am told that came about long ago because most women carry their babies on the left arm. Supposedly had to do with nursing said babies.

NO NOSE IS GOOD NOSE. That facial feature which most girls would like to have changed is the shape of the nose. Or so the surveys have indicated repeatedly. Artists recognize this fact, evidently. In a seminar on cartooning, sketch expert Bill Mauldin advised his students never to draw noses on females. The young ladies are just too sensitive about noses.

If she's a vocalist, odds run 100 to 1 she won't win the Miss America contest, remember that.

Note it repeatedly stated that animal with the biggest eyes is the blue whale. That's wrong. Some squid have eyes as big as dinner plates. Almost a foot (30 cm) in diameter.

Two out of every three single women are said to prefer pajamas to nightgowns. Three out of every four married women are known to prefer nightgowns to pajamas. And one out of every 14 women both married and single is claimed to prefer neither pajamas nor nightgowns, but no clothing at all in bed.

A mother? She is a person who, seeing there are only four pieces of apple pie for five people, promptly announces she never did care for pie.

Tenneva Jordan

MAMA NEEDS A NEW PAIR OF SHOES. Most popular games among the women who gamble at Las Vegas, in descending order, are slot machines, blackjack, roulette and dice. Were you aware the lady gamblers nationwide outnumber the men gamblers? Such was the claim of that expert John Scarne. He said about 48 million of the almost 90 million gamblers in the country are female. And it's a fact, too, that more than 10,000 women work as bookies.

Two and a half hours is about how long a woman can play the slot machines at the Nevada clubs when she's in high heels. But if she shows up in flats, she can perch there with the click and clatter for as long as four hours. So says a gambling expert who made a study of that significant matter.

HAIR

Exactly who first started using hair curling irons remains a mystery, but the record indicates the old Romans in the reign of Emperor Titus, A.D. 79 to 81, employed little hollow tubes filled with boiling water for that chore.

Someday, every man will be bald. So say the scientists. Matter of evolution. What's intriguing about this intelligence is the conviction of a few of these scholars that the bald-headed man of today is maybe a million years before his time.

The airline people have figured out that a stewardess on one round-trip Atlantic crossing walks about 10 miles (16 km).

One hundred years ago, a woman thought herself to be particularly gifted if she were one of those who grew a faint moustache. That light down on the female face was considered most attractive then.

A medical specialist says you can reckon the average 18-month-old little girl will be just about twice as tall and five times as heavy at the age of 18.

Q. What's the most weight a New York City fashion model can have now?

A. Weight isn't as significant as proportion, the agency people say. There's no specific weight limitation, as such. Height, though, is fairly standard. Between 5-foot-7 and 5-foot-9 (168 and 172 cm) is about right. And the hips and thighs are taped with some care, too. Hips over 35 inches (88 cm) are rejected. Most common hip measurement is 33 inches (83 cm).

MOST CLOTHES. What is the world's largest manufacturer of feminine apparel? No doubt it's Mattel, the toymaker, which puts out 36 new Barbie-doll outfits each year. The firm counts on an annual sale of about 20 million such costumes.

TIMES CHANGE. He was 83 years old, this convict, recently released. And he had been in prison just about all his life. A reporter asked him what impressed him most about this fabulous new world outside the walls. "The women," the old man said. "When I went to jail, women were round. Now they're oblong."

Thing about an Aries girl, claim the stargazers, is she tends to keep her youthful appearance far longer than most. It's a rare Aries who ever resorts to the surgical face lift.

Am having great difficulty accepting the claim of that marketing man who avers that 9-year-old girls in the U.S. spend approximately $2 million a year on bras. Come on.

Typically, hair grows fastest on young women when they're in their late teens and early 20's. And it grows fastest in the summer, too.

Q. Do most women get better looking after they've married?

A. Most women think so, surveys show.

Suspect you already know that when you take off or put on weight, the change is soonest apparent around the waistline. But were you aware that such a loss or gain is least apparent in the legs? No girl with good-looking legs should forget it. That's the physical characteristic least likely to change with age.

When a Scorpio woman is irritated by her husband, she's apt to cry. So is a Leo wife. The Libra girl tends to sulk, however. And the Pisces woman is inclined to deliver sarcastic remarks. Or so say the stargazers.

STAND OUT IN THE CROWD

Mister, if you want the girls to notice you, wear a red vest and a yellow tie. Such is the contention of a fellow who has made a study of color in clothing. "Put a man with such a vest and tie in a ballroom full of 150 mixed guests," he says, "and he'll not escape the attention of even one of the ladies there." No, nor would a man in scuba gear with a pink parasol.

CLEOPATRA

Young lady, do you daub perfume between each of your toes? If not, why not? It's a matter of record that Cleopatra did that.

Not many women have used perfume as extensively in their amorous pursuits as did Cleopatra. When she set out to meet Mark Antony, history records, she even sprinkled it all over the sails of her barge.

A plumbing appliance store manager put this sign up in his window: "Cast iron sinks." Thought it quaint when a lady passer-by murmured, "Everybody knows that."

The fewer the women in a department store, the more likely they'll buy something.

ON THE JOB. Numerous young ladies decline to study for a career on the theory they're simply going to get married anyway. Too bad. Fact is that high-school girl about to graduate can expect to spend 28 years of her life on some sort of payroll job outside her home.

Surely you, too, take a position on limericks, good and bad. Judge this one, please:

> Said an envious erudite ermine,
> "There's one thing I cannot determine.
>   When a dame wears my coat,
>   She's a person of note.
> When I wear it, I'm only called vermin!"

HEMLINES. Women's hemlines go up as the economy gets better. They stay put when nothing happens in commerce. They go down when business drops off. A client notes this ancient theory was verified again during the last year or so. Question is why. Nobody knows why, evidently. But the record indicates the pattern dates back more than 65 years.

POOR ANNE. Pause, please, to offer a little gentle sympathy for Anne Hathaway, the widow of Mr. William Shakespeare. Only thing she inherited from him upon his death was his "second best bed." Wait, believe there was some other incidental furniture thrown in, too. But it hardly counted, considering.

French women years ago used to strap thin slices of raw beef to their faces overnight. To ward off wrinkles. Maybe that's where the cosmetic houses got the idea to come out with a wrinkle remover made from cow's blood. Claim is it pulls skin tight for a few hours. Maybe so. You don't see many cows with wrinkles. Anyhow, it's on the market.

Q. If the tape measurements of all the Miss Americas were averaged out, what would they be?

A. 34¾—24—35¼ (87—60—88 cm).

MONUMENTS. More monuments have been erected to Buddha than to any other man. But can you name the woman for whom the most monuments have been erected? Quite so, the Virgin Mary.

RIDES. It is far easier for any woman afoot than for any male pedestrian to catch a ride in traffic, no? No, not when it comes to the roving cab drivers in big towns. They tend to pass up the little ladies to pick up the old boys every time when there's a choice, I'm told. Men tip better. Much better.

The deltoid muscle in a woman's upper arm generally is the better developed of her arm muscles, because that's the one she exercises most in fixing her hair.

FERTILITY. Women who take those pep pills known as amphetamines are more fertile than other women. Women who smoke marijuana are less fertile. Or such be the indications of medical statistics compiled in England.

THE ODDS

Young lady, where do you expect to find your future matrimonial mate? Our Love and War man reports the romance statisticians have done a little calculating about that. They say the odds run 70 to one that you won't marry any of the boys in the office where you work. About 100 to one you won't marry your boss. And 1,700 to one you won't marry your doctor.

Q. You once said the biggest reason girls got turned down for modeling jobs was circles under their eyes. What's the second biggest reason?

A. Short necks. The most-employed models have those long swan-like necks. Incidentally, you might think overweight would be a main reason for turning down models, but it's not, because rarely do overweight girls apply for such jobs.

Fellow I know claims he can identify a highly-experienced professional waitress on any crowded street just by the way she walks among the bodies. She glides, he says. Other women take short choppy steps, but the long-time waitress slips over the sidewalk like spilled cream and O. J. Simpson. He also confirms the oft-reported claim that waitresses almost invariably are good dancers.

There's a remarkable statistic that pertains to women who take up chemistry for a career. One out of every 10 deaths among them is a suicide. Can find no explanation for it, but the suicide rate among female chemists is about two and a half times as high as among male chemists. Odd.

A renowned photographer of gorgeous girls says he proposes to every model he photographs. Trick is to get them to look into the camera lens most romantically, just the way they might look into the eyes of their gentlemen friends, says he. So as he squeezes off his shots, he whispers, "You're beautiful. Will you marry me?" He thinks this does much to suddenly soften their faces.

No high school girl should forget the odds run 140,000 to one against the possibility that she'll marry one of her teachers.

Q. Wasn't it Lord Chandos who described flattery as "the food of fools?"

A. No, Jonathan Swift said that. Lord Chandos said flattery is "the infantry of negotiation."

Seven out of every ten grown-up American women tell pollsters they're not satisfied with their bust measurements.

The Virgo girl typically tends to be a perfectionist. Particularly in her requirements for gentlemen friends. She's apt to be a little standoffish, at first. But once she catches fire in romance, she burns more brightly than any. Or so say the stargazers.

Q. When did the Miss America officials ban animal acts from that beauty contest?

A. In 1949, after Carol Fraser, Miss Montana, almost got tossed into the orchestra pit at Atlantic City's Convention Hall when her palomino stumbled on stage.

One historical footnote records that Cleopatra habitually nibbled pickles as her own little health food fetish.

THOUGHTFUL LAUGHTER

That fancy French lady Coco Chanel isn't around anymore, but her lingo lingers: "Women of a certain age talk to me openly about having their faces lifted. A face of 50 should show something. If it looks like 20, empty without a line of experience, it looks moronic. Should Lincoln have had his wrinkles removed? We are born with one face, but laughing or crying, wisely or otherwise, eventually we form our own lines. A good face is composed of thoughtful laughter."

13 Those Untiring
Medical Researchers

Don't know how they found out, but the men of science insist no dog ever gets bored.

First of the five senses to develop in a human being is sense of smell.

FINGERS. Is your third finger nearly as long as your second? If so, odds are you're a taker of chances, a gambler. Or such be the claim of a theorist who contends that physical characteristics denote personality traits. This is the same savant who says a straight little finger suggests the possessor has not just one but several distinct talents.

Q. How hot should a sauna bath be? How long should you stay in it?

A. Women in the U.S. seem to like it at about 175 degrees F. (79 degrees C.). Men are said to prefer approximately 200 degrees F. (93 degrees C.). Might mention that some Finns are known to heat it up to as much as 248 degrees F. (120 degrees C.). That's too hot. Medicos say a citizen would do well to stay in a sauna no less than five minutes and no more than 15 minutes.

Here's a little tip for that man who loathes the shock of stepping into a cold shower or sitting down in a cold bath or wading into a cold swimming pool. Exhale slowly. For intricate reasons too lengthy for this space, letting the breath out in a controlled manner helps the body adjust to the shivery shift in temperature. Might try that.

RUSSIAN SLEEP. Was in 1948 that doctors in the Soviet Union came up with something called electro-sleep. They taped electrodes to the eyelids and mastoids of volunteers to send mild currents through their heads. Both tensions and anxieties promptly went away, those experimenters reported, and said volunteers dozed right off. American researchers now are thinking about trying to put anti-insomnia machines on the market.

Dental experts now get around to telling us that the time of day when the brushing of the teeth does the least good is just before breakfast.

If you stripped absolutely all the fat off both a piece of pork and a piece of beef, you couldn't taste the difference. Such is the surprising claim of U.S. Department of Agriculture researchers.

SMOKING

The Tobacco Institute financed research in Southern California wherefrom came the announcement that brain-wave devices prove that cigarette smokers think more than nonsmokers. Surprised?

But the men of science haven't quite pinned down why chain smokers have far more family fights than nonsmokers. They're working on it.

PEACHES AND SOUP. What cling peaches and chicken soup have in common is noteworthy, I think. Something about their molecular structure lets them get hotter than most other foods and stay hotter longer.

So you're feeling unusually tired, are you? Having trouble making up your mind about something important? That may explain it. Medicos contend prolonged indecision almost invariably brings on that fagged-out feeling.

DANCERS. Among medical men, the best dancers are the psychoanalysts. So claims a student of the matter. The analysts themselves agree, he says. Understand they generally admit they enjoy skittering around the dance floor because they like the attention of the whole room. Most other doctors dance rarely. The dancing surgeon is almost unheard of.

In the case of Siamese twins, one is right-handed, the other left-handed, always. Or so a doctor tells me.

PERSPIRATION. Medical researchers now say that perspiration doesn't get rid of bodily poisons, contrary to longheld belief. Perspiration, they say, is nothing but sterile water with some dissolved salts in it.

Emotions, not the heat of the day, account for most perspiration.

HEADACHES

It's the unmarried girl under the age of 21 who's statistically most inclined to get a headache.

It's a proven fact, too, that few patients in mental hospitals ever get headaches.

How the medical researchers found this out is a mystery, but they insist that no animal besides man gets headaches.

109

HANDEDNESS TEST. Hold up your thumbs side by side to look at the base of their nails, please. On which thumb is the nail wider and squarer? If the left, you're left-handed. If the right, right-handed. A Missouri medical fellow discovered this handedness test. If you already knew whether you were left-handed or right-handed, never mind.

Q. How often do you bump into somebody who gets a bad reaction to penicillin?

A. It upsets one in ten, seriously sickens one in 2,500, kills one in 100,000.

STOP SHAVING. Statistically, men with light beards appear to be more susceptible to heart attacks than men with heavy beards, researchers now say.

It has been determined scientifically that the most efficient sweepers use brooms with handles 6 inches (15 cm) longer than those sweepers are tall.

PARADISE LOST

That island called Grand Cayman lies midway between Jamaica and Cuba. Most of its 6,000 natives are the white descendants of pirates and other seafaring souls. They go to church with great regularity and drink a lot of liquor. They pay no income or real estate taxes. The water around them is calm and clear and warm, and orchids grow all over their land. A paradise, really. Recent medical studies indicate the two major ailments there are hypertension and anxiety neuroses.

Your blood completes a circuit of your body every 23 seconds.

THIRST

What sort of drink actually works best to quench your thirst? That's what the science boys wanted to know. So they proved first that the quench-quotient depends on high water content. Plain water itself, therefore, ranks No. 1. Their ranking of other beverages: Club soda, No. 2. Iced tea, No. 3. Coffee, No. 4. Diet cola, No. 5. Presweetened Kool-Aid, No. 6. Beer, No. 7. Ginger ale, No. 8. Milk, No. 9.

One authority who ought to know contends the world's best thirst quencher is *not* plain water, but rather tomato juice mixed half and half with water. Nothing else so quickly replaces lost body fluids, it's averred.

Did I tell you only about one out of every 50 cases of Rocky Mountain spotted fever crops up in the Rocky Mountains?

Maybe your scales don't show it, but the fact is your body changes its weight from minute to minute.

DIETING

The best way to lose weight is to curb the appetite by eating an apple half an hour before every meal.

One certain way to lose weight, another claims, is to wait two minutes between bites.

NEARSIGHTED. Scientists tested 17,000 British children who were 11 years old. And the testers found that the nearsighted children appeared on the average to be about a year ahead of the overall group in such matters as arithmetic and general ability. A check then of their records showed that even at age 7, before they'd been fitted with glasses, they'd exhibited higher-than-average intelligence.

To allow a child to walk at too early an age is to encourage bowleggedness. That is the ancient belief of numerous citizens. Horseradish, says psychologist Philip R. Zelazo, or words to that effect. He blames wrong food, mostly. Says early walking is dandy for the muscles.

Maybe you don't realize it takes longer to become a dermatologist than to become a pediatrician.

Medical studies show children do not tend to be as vulnerable to poisonous snakebite as do adults for some peculiar reason.

Presume you weigh 40 times as much as your brain, sir. That's average.

RED

Quick, name any one color that leaps to mind! Put that command to 50 people. Just about 30 of them will say, "Red." Or so the psychology scholars report.

Some baby experts say red is the only color that stirs up a strong reaction in infants.

That Soviet Union mastermind known as Lenin died in 1924. Numerous scientists asked the Russian government for permission to analyze his brain. So many scientists did so, in fact, that the brain was cut into 31,000 pieces.

BEARDS. Some men of science claim they've proved their beards grow most on Wednesdays and least on Sundays. What explains it, they say, is the contention that weekend pursuits—drinking, dining out, romance—inhibit beard growth slightly. Fascinating, if factual.

Q. How can I find out how much blood I have?

A. Divide your weight by 12. That's how many pints.

Look in the mirror, if you will. Is the right side of your face more strongly developed than the left? Such be the case in 96 out of every 100 citizens, according to the medicos.

Age 10 is said to be when your hearing reaches its peak of keenness.

Age 10 is also that year of life when the average person sees best. Further, it's the safest year of life, statistically.

How do you account for the fact that more boys are born in the summer and more girls in the winter? A scholar named Herman M. Slatis of McGill University in Montreal claims such to be the case.

Why people tend to lose their ability to blush when they get into their 30's is another medical mystery.

Do you believe some faith healers really can cure physical ailments? If not, how do you explain that remarkable experiment undertaken by McGill University. Two batches of sick white mice were put in separate cages. Selected faith healers prayed over one cage, but not over the other. The prayed-over mice reportedly got well far more quickly than did the ignored mice. The devout like to cite this report. Skeptics contend any sick animal's chances of recovery improve when it gets a lot of attention.

Am asked the usual approximate weight of the head of a 185-pound (83 kg) man. Ah, the things a fellow has to do to satisfy the customer! All right, that head weighs 13 pounds (5.9 kg).

Best exercise to keep in good physical condition is roller skating. No, I didn't say that. A U.S. Olympic team doctor named Max Novich said it.

Foot doctors say the best time of day to buy a pair of shoes is late afternoon.

Q. How long does it take a fingernail to be replaced completely from base to tip?

A. Figure four to five months.

BEST TEMPERATURES. At what air temperature do people do their best work? Depends on the sort of work. Mental, around 40 degrees F. (4.4 degrees C.). Physical, about 65 degrees F. (18.3 degrees C.). That's what the medicos report, at any rate. Already mentioned that they say human fertility is highest when the air temperature stands at 64 degrees F. (17.8 degrees C.).

The acid inside your midsection is so strong, say the medical men, it would blister the palm of your hand.

That baby girls at birth are about a month ahead of boys in physical development has been reported. But now some medical men have added another footnote. There's evidence, they say, that girls before birth are not carried quite so long by their mothers as are boys. This gets clinical, doesn't it? Let's quit for the day.

14 Words and Meanings

A "spoonerism" is defined by the language specialists as "an unintentional transposition of word and thought." Like: "I remember your name perfectly, but I just can't think of your face." It was William Archibald Spooner of New College, Oxford, who uttered that line and many another. But one of his more spectacular, I think, he delivered to a small group of girls in a large auditorium full of hard seats at a women's college. Began he: "What am I to tell this audience of beery wenches?"

Flammable and inflammable mean the same. Tolerable and intolerable mean the opposite. Loosen and unloosen mean the same. Fasten and unfasten mean the opposite. Odd, what? Any others?

Q. Why is a book of maps called an atlas?

A. Because practically all the early map books started out with frontispieces that pictured the mythical character Atlas holding the world on his back. It was slang, originally. Like Ma Bell. Or GI. Or cop.

TIGER RAG. Lowest hand a man can hold in ordinary draw poker is a seven high, deuce low, with no pair, straight or flush. And such a hand in the lingo of yesteryear's jazz was known as a tiger. You recall that jazz piece called "Tiger Rag?" It refers not to the big striped cat, but to the lowest possible poker hand. So reports our Language man.

The Comanche's word for "horse" translated as "God dog."

In the lingo of the Old West's cowpunchers, an orphaned calf was not a "dogie," but a "leppy." A "dogie" was a weak calf.

SHOELACE. Will bet you a quarter on the corner that nobody at the dinner table tonight can tell you the name of that little metal or plastic tip on the end of a shoelace. It's an aglet.

That word "Hallelujah" is common to all languages. It's never translated.

Q. What's "hula" mean in Hawaiian?

A. Simply, "dancing."

The three most useful languages for research scientists now, in descending order, are said to be: 1. English. 2. Russian. 3. German.

WORDS, WORDS, WORDS. Did you speak 4,800 words yet today? If not, better get with it. That's said to be the average word delivery daily of the typical conversationalist.

Am repeatedly asked if "I" is among the 10 most frequently written words in English. It is. The other nine are: the, of, and, to, a, in, that, is, it.

The early U.S. colonists didn't much cotton to the English custom of addressing an employer as "master." Much preferred was the Dutch word "baas" meaning "uncle." That's where the word "boss" comes from.

HAWAIIAN. Be seated, class, and open your primers to the Hawaiian alphabet: A, E, H, I, K, L, M, N, O, P, U and W. Every Hawaiian word ends with a vowel. So does every syllable. Consonants never occur without a vowel between them. And in most every Hawaiian word, the accent falls on the next to last syllable.

The letters "I.O.U." didn't originally mean "I owe you." They meant "I owe unto" followed by the creditor's name.

Q. What does "getting a Valentine" mean in criminal jargon?

A. Receiving a one-year jail sentence.

Q. What's the difference between crud and goop?

A. Moisture content. It isn't goop unless it's wet, but crud can be completely dry. Sort of like the difference between trash and slop. I don't want to talk about it anymore.

Language scholars say they've turned up one African tribe that speaks a tongue quite similar to that of the American Cherokee Indian. And they're now convinced that those Africans somehow learned it from the Indians, not vice versa.

Q. Wasn't "In God We Trust" on the very first U.S. coin ever issued?

A. No, the motto on that coin, a penny, minted in 1787, was "Mind Your Own Business."

Item 418B in our Language man's file reads: "English is the language to swear in, French the language to converse in, Italian the language to sing in, Spanish the language to pray and to make love in, and German the language to drive hogs in."

The quaint conversationalists now refer to junk food as "kiddie litter."

The big book at hand defines a "canard" as "an extravagant or absurd report or story set afloat to delude the public." Comes from the French word meaning "duck." Tale behind it is a Frenchman once bet he could eat 20 ducks at one sitting, if given 20 days to prepare for the banquet. He didn't win his bet. Instead, he fed one duck a day to others, dining on the last one himself on the 20th day. But the nonsense drew a lot of attention, so the word for duck came to mean a phony report.

Q. Mark Twain's writing refers now and then to a "hogshead." What's that?

A. A wooden cask that holds 63 gallons (239 liters). Bigger than an ordinary barrel.

HARD TO SWALLOW. The original pumpernickel bread was said to create gas in the innards of Satan. And the word pumpernickel, in fact, comes from an early high German set of syllables that meant the Devil's gas, or something similar.

Q. What's a drupe?

A. That's any fruit with its seed in a stone. Like a peach or a cherry or an olive.

There's no bone in whalebone, no rice in rice paper and no kid in kid gloves, remember that.

Here's a kindly client who identifies himself as well as me as a "spermologer." Looked it up. "A collector of trivial data." Correct. Anybody who knows what a spermologer is, is one.

That word "paradise" originally was the Persian word for a royal amusement park.

If called upon to name a word with one vowel repeated six times, say "indivisibility."

Another of those relatively rare words with opposite meanings, please note, is dust. As in dust the crops in one instance and dust the piano in another. Cleave is such a word, too.

COURTING

You know how an amorous bachelor is said to "court" the object of his affection? Client asks why that's so called. If you wanted something from a king in the 1400's on, you had to hang around his courtyard until he took the notion to check out your action. If you hung around long enough, you were

119

said to pay "court" to His Highness. Our Language man says sardonic conversationalists eventually spun off the expression to apply to young fellows who hung around their selected girls.

MINIVER. Rare is the Seasoned Citizen hereabouts who doesn't recall that English fictional character known as Mrs. Miniver. Less widely known is the significance of the name Miniver. The word originally identified that ermine fur which royalty wore to identify rank.

Our word "infant" comes from the Latin word meaning "unable to speak."

The sound "a" as in father is common to all languages.

Q. Is E the most frequently used letter in other languages as well as in English?

A. In French, Italian and Spanish it is. In Portuguese, A is first, then E.

KANGAROO. "Kan-ga-roo" in the native Kanaka dialect means "I don't know." Story goes that an early English explorer asked an Australian native what those oddball animals were. And the native replied, "kan-ga-roo." Shrug.

WRITING ON THE WALL. No doubt you knew that writings on walls are called "graffiti," but did you also know that just one writing on just one wall is called a "graffito?"

Couple more words, each of which bears two exactly opposite meanings, are citation and sanction.

Our language man once reported that "purple" is a word that does not rhyme with any other words. To it, he now adds "silver," "spirit" and "chimney," "liquid," "window" and "carpet." Any others?

If you can't stand children, sir, your particular affliction is called misopedia.

FOX. Please bear in mind, too, the flying fox is not a fox but a bat. Hudson Bay is not a bay but an inland sea, wormwood is not a wood but an herb, the white whale is not a whale but a sturgeon, and as you know, the funny bone is not a bone but a nerve.

Q. How big a vocabulary has the average 2-year-old?

A. Just 272 words, say the experts.

Q. Why is whiskey so called?

A. Comes from the Irish *usquedaugh* meaning "water of life."

Q. Why is the Soviet Union's "Kremlin" so called?

A. Means "fortress" in Russian.

All Japanese words end in vowels or the letter N.

Not many realize that the name of Spain originally meant "land of the rabbit."

As to that meaning of the name "Alaska," am told it comes from an Indian word *alayeksha* meaning "the grand land" or "the mainland."

IS IT SO? Our Language man nominates this as the most significant 10-word sentence of all wherein each word contains only two letters: "If it is to be, it is up to me." Quite so, quite so. Post it on the blackboard, professor.

In Arabic, *al* meant "the" and *manakh* meant "weather." Somebody put the two together to make "almanac."

Q. What's a "dactylogram?"

A. A fingerprint.

The word "stepson" came into the language long before the word "stepfather." And the "step" in the original word came from the old English "steop" meaning bereaved.

Q. Where'd we get the word "succotash?"

A. From the Narraganset Indian word *meseckquatash*. Originally, it was a boiled stew of venison, fish and Indian corn. A combination of beans and corn is sufficient succotash now, though.

"Supercilious" comes from Latin words meaning "over" and "eyelid." Something like "high brow." You know how the haughty raise their eyebrows to show disdain? That's supercilious.

122

What letter of the alphabet is pronounced in the most ways? How about "u?" It sounds different in busy, bury, thud, beautiful, burr, bull and buy.

Am repeatedly asked the origin of the name "California." Much debate about that. But most historians now think it came from an old Spanish romance written by Montalvo in 1510. A fictional island so named therein was described as a paradise that glittered with gold and jewels. Cortez was first to apply the name to the real southern California area, it's believed.

Q. Why do we call the "guitar" by that name?

A. Comes from the Greek word *kithara* which was the national instrument of ancient Greece. A lot of people don't realize how old the guitar really is. Were you aware that Benjamin Franklin was something of a virtuoso on the guitar?

The original calico came from the town of Calicut in India. No, not Calcutta. Calicut.

At the moment, can only think of one word—latchstring—containing six consecutive consonants. Must be others, though.

You know the avocado used to be called the alligator pear, but were you aware that avocado is a corruption of the Spanish word *abuacat* meaning alligator?

Can't find the word "octothorp" in any dictionary, but a helpful client insists it's the official name for that numbers sign that looks like this: #.

Q. Why do the Scots sometimes refer to the moon as "MacFarlane's Lantern?"

A. A family named MacFarlane in the 19th century grew infamous thereabouts, working mostly by night, stealing cattle.

"Orphan: A living person whom death has deprived of the power of filial gratitude." Who said that?

What two words did you first learn to read? Not speak, read. An educator of some renown contends "corn" and "flakes" probably merit that distinction. For most people. He says the majority of youngsters learn to read cereal boxes long before children's stories.

DIRTY SHIRTS. The word "shirt" was unspeakable in polite society 150 years ago. But "smock" was all right. Mysteriously, then "smock" came to be regarded as vulgar. So "shift" suddenly grew popular. Eventually, "shift" became disreputable, and by the turn of the century, it couldn't be spoken in public. But "shirt" was finally quite acceptable. I don't get it.

Q. The so-called "long dozen," sometimes called the "baker's dozen," is 13. What's a "long hundred?"

A. That's 120.

Q. In the lingo of the Latins, what does *onces* mean?

A. That translates "elevenses." Refers to the 11 a.m. coffee break. That morning coffee break has become almost as popular in South America as the English tea time.

In the old Anglo-Saxon lingo, the word *ang* meant "painful" and *naegl* means "nail." That's the origin of "hangnail," reports our Language man.

In Choctaw, that word *Oklahoma* means "people red."

Q. Only three words in English end with the letters "gry." Angry. Hungry. And what's the third?

A. Puggry, a scarf worn around a pith helmet by the British in India. That's sort of cheating, though. Not only is puggry obscure, but it's spelled in various ways.

What, you can't name the only three current words in English that begin with the letters "dw?" Spring that one on the family scholar. Reply should be dwarf, dwell, and dwindle.

Q. Why is the city of Toronto so called?

A. Comes from a Huron Indian word meaning either "place of plenty" or "meeting."

A ball of yarn in the early Anglo-Saxon lingo was called a *cleoven*. Clue, for short. It was said that the only way to find your route home out of some caverns was to follow back a strand of yarn you'd unraveled as you went in. The word "clue" comes from that.

A rap, as in the phrase "not worth a rap," was a counterfeit half-penny coin in 18th century Ireland.

15 Kill the Umpire

"Kill the umpire!" That's the venerable cry of the baseball fans. Question arises as to whether any umpire actually has been killed by irate fans. Just about. Umpire Billy Evans almost died after he was beaned by a bottle thrown from the stands in St. Louis. He was a borderline bed case for three weeks.

Among baseball umpires, those who lead the most dangerous lives are the Japanese. Specifically, umpires who officiate at games of that team known as the Hiroshima Carps. A sports statistician says his records reveal more Carp umpires are attacked by irate fans than umpires anywhere else worldwide.

Don't forget, half the grownups in Switzerland can ski.

ANT HILL. His golf ball landed on an ant hill. He swung, must have bashed 1,000 ants, but missed the ball. Swung again, and there sailed another 1,000 ants, but the ball stayed put. This went on. Finally, one of the dozen remaining ants looked at the rest and said, "Listen, you guys, if we want to survive, we'd better get on the ball." I don't ordinarily much go in for talking-insect stories, but thought you might be able to use this one at the next board meeting.

Howard Cosell's mother says he started talking when he was nine months old.

ARMS AND KNEES

It has been widely reported that the part of a football quarterback's body most prone to injury is the knee. And of a baseball pitcher's body, the arm, certainly. But it should also be reported that the knee and the arm of the normal person are those parts of the body far less likely than most to show any degeneration over the years. A study of the bodies of 113 persons who died at an average age of 71 indicates such. Clearly, football quarterbacks and baseball pitchers engage in unnatural practices.

WATCH OUT. Five most dangerous sports, in order, are football, skiing, baseball, swimming and basketball. Or so the researchers for a major insurance company report. The next five most dangerous, they say, are beach games, bicycling, outings at parks, golf and horseback riding. Fishing ranks thirteenth, hunting sixteenth.

That ardent conservationist John James Audubon didn't paint live birds, only birds he himself had shot.

CONDUCTORS

Clearly, a conductor of a symphony orchestra must be an athlete. Medical tests on conductors with the Cleveland Symphony Orchestra show their pulse rates rise to as much as 165 and even 195 beats per minute during some exuberant performances. And this strenuous exercise goes on for as long as 20 minutes. Believe you're aware that symphony conductors tend to live longer than do most people, no? Does the foregoing explain it?

WHO'S ON FIRST BASS? How many words can you think of that are common both to music and baseball? Like run, pitch, slide, score and tie. And if you want to play with the spellings, add base and bass.

FINE FOR BALL PLAYING. In Wenatchee, Washington, it's against the law to play baseball in a public place. In fact, it's against the law to play any kind of ball in a street. Even simple catch. That law is so broad there you can't legally toss an apple to and fro in an alley.

WRESTLERS. Don't suppose anybody pays attention to it, but the law in Los Angeles prohibits a wrestler from making faces during a match.

Did you know all the baseballs used in the major leagues here are sewn up in Haiti?

BOXERS

Quick, name that one sport wherein neither the participants nor the spectators know either the score or the winner until the contest is ended. Sure enough it's boxing.

Relatively rare is the fellow whose nerves are so constructed that he feels no pain from cuts, bruises, broken bones. But as you might guess, prize fighting attracts these abnormal men more than does any other occupation, studies show. Researchers tested 97 boxers in New York City sometime back, and 87 of them proved to be afflicted, or blessed, whichever, with this odd insensitivity.

Three out of four professional boxers who have fought more than 60 bouts show at least some symptoms of that ailment called punch drunkenness.

Name those nations who've had world's heavyweight boxing champions. All right, besides the United States, there were Great Britain with Bob Fitzsimmons, Canada with Tommy

Burns, Germany with Max Schmeling, Italy with Primo Carnera and Sweden with Ingemar Johansson.

Q. What's a "Bangor tiger"?

A. That's what the Maine woodsmen used to call any lumberjack who was particularly tricky in a log-birling contest.

SWIMMING. Was reported the ideal temperature of water for a swimming race is 76 degrees F. (24.4 degrees C.). Am asked why. Colder water stiffens a swimmer's muscles, it's said. Warmer water over-relaxes them.

Q. Didn't Joe Namath want to go to Notre Dame rather than Alabama?

A. Until he found out Notre Dame then was all boys, he did, says he.

OXYGEN

You've seen that football player on the bench with an oxygen mask over his face? Except maybe for the psychological uplift, he's not helping himself much. Medical researchers now contend that breathing oxygen before or after exercise has no effect on performance or recovery.

Q. When the pro football teams go from city to city, do they just reserve tickets on scheduled flights or do they charter airplanes?

A. They charter. From scheduled airlines.

TAXI SQUAD. In the matter of how the standby players of a football team came to be called the taxi squad: A former owner of the Cleveland Browns once owned a taxicab company. His club couldn't support the extra players, but he needed them. So he put them to work, driving his taxis. Thus the term.

Almost half the golf carts sold in this country are made in Poland where there are no golf courses.

Q. What's tennis player Evonne Goolagong's name mean?

A. Comes from the aborigine for "nose of the kangaroo."

Recently asked a math teacher, who also happens to be the high school's basketball coach, what sort of student made the best grades in his algebra classes. He said: "Always a girl, and particularly one with a real tall brother."

STRONG AS A BULL. You've heard of the fellow who trained himself to pick up a full grown bull by lifting the beast daily from the time it was born. But can you name that athlete? Milo of Crotona, he was. In the Olympic games of the Sixth Century B.C., he set a world's record by lugging a 4-year-old bull on his shoulders the length of the stadium. Or so the historical footnotes report.

Q. What kind of bathing suit did Martha Washington wear?

A. Looked sort of like a nightgown with elbow-length sleeves, a high neck and lead weights sewn into the hem at the ankles. Don't know how she kept from sinking in that thing.

That word "gymnasium" comes from the Greek *gymnos* meaning "naked." Why? Because that's how the athletes of old Greece worked out. In the nude. Garments, they thought, got in the way.

In Siberia's Verkhoyansk, nobody exercises outdoors on purpose, not in the winter. Perspiration can be dangerous. Can freeze so fast it frostbites.

HE DOES IT WITH MIRRORS. That dandy actor of yesteryear, Gary Cooper, was right-handed. But he once played the part of the great left-handed Yankee Lou Gehrig. Client wants to know how that was possible. Nothing to it. The film director reversed the club initials on Cooper's uniform, photographed him at third base instead of first, then reversed the negatives.

Q. How long does it take to make a billiard ball?

A. No doubt you mean a superior ball. Depends. They're baked in ovens. A cue ball, seven days. A solid, a little longer. A stripe, 15 days.

A two-week school for cocktail waitresses in Los Angeles includes a half-day course in karate.

AILMENT. Listed among the medical ailments of 100 years ago was a dour complaint called "mental firmentation." Its symptoms were too various to list here. But what doctors usually prescribed to cure it was bicycle riding.

BICYCLING. Question arises as to how high a bicycle seat should be set. Easy to figure. Put the left pedal at its lowest position. Sitting straight, put the left heel on that pedal. At the correct saddle height, the left knee then should be slightly bent.

That lawn game you and I call "croquet" started out in France as *paille-maille* before it turned up in England as "pall-mall."

Average professional football squad outweighs the average college squad by 2,500 pounds (1,125 kg). And the average college squad outweighs the average high school squad by 2,000 pounds (900 kg).

Football spectators hereabouts are pretty enthusiastic all right. But they're not as wild as those South American soccer audiences. To protect one particularly popular player named Maracano, the builders of the big field in Rio de Janeiro put a 9-foot (2.7 m) moat around it.

A basketball player's hearing is rarely as keen at the end of a game as at the beginning. Nothing mysterious about this. A little light exercise sharpens the sensitivity of the ears. But extremely heavy exercise tends to dull same.

Q. Has any big league baseball pitcher ever actually killed a hitter with a wild pitch?

A. Happened only once. The great Carl Mays fatally injured Ray Chapman of the Cleveland Indians in such a manner on Aug. 16, 1920. Was the only field death in all major league history.

Q. I know the Japanese like baseball, but how about football?

A. Football just flatout hasn't made it there, regret to report. Promoters introduced it over 40 years ago. But the fans shrugged. General criticism was that the huddle between each play wasted too much time.

Am advised that each of the major soccer teams in Africa has its own witch doctor.

RIOT

Small riots occur from time to time at sporting events, as everybody knows, over the decisions of referees and umpires. But no riot in the last 1,443 years compares with the big fight during a chariot race in the Hippodrome of Constantinople. Name of the character who made the unpopular ruling remains unknown. What is known is most of the city was destroyed and 30,000 citizens were killed.

Q. Is it true that Howard Cosell and Joe Garagiola have a running feud going?

A. Not exactly. They don't pay much attention to each other. I don't know what Howard says about Joe, but Joe says about

Howard: "I consider Cosell a flunk-out lawyer. If he had breakfast, lunch and dinner with everybody he says he does, he'd weigh 673 pounds."

Q. Who invented boxing gloves?

A. Fellow named Jack Broughton. Little over 200 years ago. But they were for practice only. The real fights were bare-fisted then. That is, modern boxing gloves. Ancient Greek boxers wrapped their fists in strips of leather studded with lead plates. Rematches were rare.

RING. Why is a boxing ring called a "ring" when it's square? Because the original boxing sites were simply circles drawn with sticks in the dirt. Believe I already told you that the earlier boxers sat not on stools, but on the knees of their handlers.

Exercise is good for your bones as well as for your muscles. The tug of the muscles against the bones strengthens them. The medical specialist who reports the foregoing contends it's particularly important after the age of 40 when the bones tend to get thinner and more brittle.

Q. Do you play golf, Louie?

A. No, sir, gave it up. Last time out—that was in Seattle—I happened to drop the innocent remark, "Don't seem to be playing my usual game today." And the caddy said, "What game do you usually play, mister?" That did it.

PHOTO FINISH

Instant replay on TV surprisingly has proved umpires and referees are far more often right than wrong in their play calls. In light of this, inquires a client, didn't the photo finish camera in horseracing prove the judges were more often right than wrong in naming winners? Certainly. Still, judges in 1935, before the camera, acknowledged only 20 dead heats.

But in 1938 after most tracks had cameras, the films recorded 264 dead heats. Clearly, thousands of close finishes had been miscalled previously.

Five out of six race horses cost more to train than they ever earn. And almost all the rest barely break even. But there are those few, those fabulous few! Did I tell you 32 people paid $190,000 each for a share in the breeding career of Secretariat?

Wilt Chamberlain's bathtub holds 20 times more water than a normal tub.

SUPERSTITIONS

Which do you put on first, your left sock or your right? That's what I asked. "Your right," reports a kindly client, "if you're an old-time professional baseball player. Superstition among just about all the ball players required them to do everything from the right side first. Right sock first, right shoe first, shave on the right side first, right leg into the pants first. Winning games depended on it."

That great superstitious fistfighter of yesteryear, John L. Sullivan, never allowed himself to enter the ring ahead of his opponent. By never, I mean almost. One fighter, who knew all about old John's fear of the jinx, tricked him. This cunning character preceded Sullivan to ringside, then turned back at the last moment. Sullivan found himself through the ropes first. And 21 rounds later, that savvy soul, Gentleman Jim Corbett, was world champ. Told you, didn't I, that throughout his entire fighting career, Corbett never got a black eye or a bloody nose? That, too, is true.

Those sumo wrestlers in Japan chew up a lot of time in the preliminary ritual, but the actual match only lasts on the average about 10 seconds.

Q. Who has to be in better physical condition, a football player or a boxer?

135

A. The boxer, no doubt about it. In a 10-round boxing match, at three minutes per round, the boxer supposedly works at full speed contact for a total of 30 minutes. But in a football game the average player actually works at full-speed contact for only about 10 minutes.

Tests show the IQs of most football players rank in the top 25 per cent.

FOOTBALL. Sports doctors report as many as 50,000 non-professional football players undergo surgery each autumn for knee and ankle injuries.

Any good basketball athlete who plays all four quarters without a substitute can be expected to run about 5 miles (8 km) during a game.

Q. Not counting the warmup throws, how many pitches are made in the average nine-inning baseball game?

A. Figure 250.

When Japanese fishermen started using pink nets, they boosted their catches by 60 per cent. They wondered why. Still do. Me too.

HUNTER OR HUNTED

Question arises as to whether man among the land animals throughout history has been primarily the hunter or the hunted. In other words, predator or prey. That's easy. Look at his eyes. They're set on the front of his head. That's a distinguishing characteristic among predatory beasts. Tigers, for instance. The eyes of defensive animals tend to be set on the sides of the heads, swiveling in such a manner so as to see in many directions at one time. Horses, for instance. There are even those who claim men with close-set eyes make the best hunters. But that's a little much.

PITCHING ELEPHANTS

Of all the animals in the world, including man, that mammal which can throw a baseball the fastest, if properly taught, is said to be the elephant. A Ceylonese pachyderm named Susie in the zoo at Independence, Kansas, can throw a projectile with the speed of a bullet. I make specific reference to a baseball, not because Susie has yet been trained as a reliever, but because a baseball is the most obvious thing you're supposed to throw fast. However, it's expected that pitching elephants in the future will do for the game of baseball what boxing kangaroos 50 years ago did for prize fighting. Nothing.

Believe I told you that marine scientists have trained porpoises to throw footballs as far as 60 feet (18 m). But did I mention that they throw perfect spirals?

EX-FIGHTERS

Scholars checked out the later careers of 95 professional prizefighters. Each had been either a champion or a major contender. Each had earned more than $100,000 in the ring. They wound up as: Laborers, mostly in steel mills, 18; wrestlers, 2; tavern bouncers, bartenders or owners, 28; janitors, 2; bookies, 3; taxi drivers, 3; house painters, 18; newsstand tenders, 3; liquor salesmen, 2; gas station owners or attendants, 2; tailor, 1; race track hands, 3; businessman whose business wasn't explained, 1; and fight trainers or managers, the rest.

In Burma lives a tribe of athletes called the Intha who row their longboats not with their arms but with their legs.

It's not enough to mention Notre Dame's rowing team had a member named Roe. Must report also that team had at the same time a fellow called Orr.

If you don't think the folks in the grandstand influence the boys on the field, consider the fact that the home team wins three times as many football games as the visiting team.

It's claimed by those who should know that the mustard you put on your hot dog tends to slow down your heartbeat.

A hotel bellboy of lengthy experience now contends dentists rank way down there with professional baseball players and politicians as the poorest tippers.

Far more men than women suffer back pains, and far more former athletes than non-athletes do likewise. Or so the medicos report.

OUCH. Only one out of every 20 professional football players comes out of a game unbruised. More specifically, eight out of 20 get big bruises. And 11 out of 20, little bruises.

Count up the wounded in hunting accidents—39 per cent are lads from 16 to 19 years old. Count up those who fire the guns in such accidents—46 per cent are boys the same age.

Please note, approximately 93 per cent of the people who go swimming every summer can't swim more than 40 yards (36 m) at a stretch, if at all.

In Louisville, Kentucky, it's against the law to shoot a fish with a bow and arrow, so watch that.

16 How High Can a Flea Jump?

Credit the flea as the best of all jumpers. It has been known to jump 13 inches (32 cm). Proportionately, if the flea were as big as a man with its power still intact, it could long-jump 500 feet and high-jump 300.

But now am told the record high jump for a flea is exactly 7 inches (17.5 cm). Shrug.

A kindly client insists you'll eliminate any fleas brought into your house by the family pet if you place a few green walnuts under chairs, beds and around said pet's sleeping areas. Interesting, if true.

Vegetarians like to point out that the oldest living animal, the giant turtle, eats no meat. Likewise, the elephant, which also survives longer than most animals. And it's true, too, of the birds that hold the old-age records.

DUST BATHS

Customer inquires as to why birds take dust baths. That's no mystery. Dust absorbs the excess oil on their feathers. If they didn't dust themselves with some regularity, they'd eventually get too oily to fly in a fancy manner.

ANTS

Seem to recall that the ants in the Pacific Northwest where I grew up tended to travel in straight lines. But the ants down in sunny Texas more frequently appear to scatter when they move. Suddenly comes an explanation. A bug expert who ought to know insists that ants queue up when rain is expected, but wander all over the place when fair weather is in the offing.

Eggs of some of the earthworms in Australia look like big olives.

One year of a horse's life equals about three years of a man's life. Or so the experts aver. Interesting, if true. If the Kentucky Derby were a foot race of boys and girls instead of horses, the contestants would only be about nine years old. If Secretariat were a young man instead of a stallion, he would have been put out to stud at about the age of 12.

That bee known as the Royal Mayan doesn't sting, it bites.

APPLES. The orchard boys in Sweden have polished up their science to such a degree that 2-pound (.9-kg) apples there are not now unusual.

I like trees, because they seem more resigned to the way they have to live than other things do.

Willa Cather

A mole in a tunnel can go either direction at just about the same speed without turning around. Its fur has no grain. Lies forward as easily as backward. If there's any other land animal that can romp along in reverse as fast as in high gear straight ahead, I can't name it. Can you?

You didn't know a cow can transmit rabies, did you?

140

Honeybees follow a timetable in their calls on flowers. Dandelions, about 9 a.m. Cornflowers, about 11 a.m. Red clover, about 1 p.m. Evidently, these blooms release more nectar at certain hours.

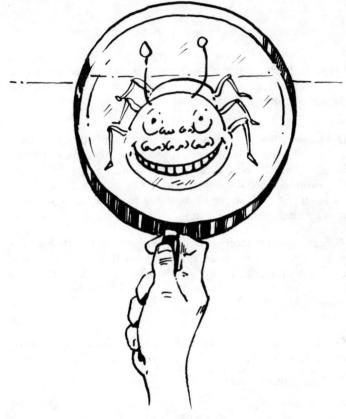

Am advised an ordinary ant has five noses each designated to smell a different odor.

That beast known as the banded anteater devours from 10,000 to 20,000 termites a day, and nothing else.

Q. Both watermelons and peanuts are native to Africa, no?

A. Watermelon, yes. Peanuts, no. The Bantu tribe of Africa imported the first peanuts from South America. Slave traders then introduced them into the Jamestown colony here. The Bantus called them *nguba,* incidentally, which is where we got the name "goober."

The feathers of a pigeon weigh more than its bones.

Frogs prefer the color blue. They'll jump toward blue every time. Rather than to green or black or orange. Such is the dubious claim of a biology researcher.

Did I ever tell you a crocodile can't swim without rolling over and over unless it swallows enough rocks to counterbalance its tail? And the weight of the rock ballast is always in precise ratio to the tail weight. A few croc experts are so savvy they can just look at one of those big beasts and tell you how many pounds of rocks are in it.

A cat's digestive tract is four times the length of its body. A goat's digestive tract is 26 times the length of its body. How come the difference? Why, sir, there's always that sort of difference between the carnivorous animal and the vegetation eater.

Q. How long does it take a skunk to manufacture an ounce of that foul odor?

A. Figure three weeks.

RABBIT EARS

Do you know why a rabbit has long ears? Wait, don't call that a ridiculous query. A scholar at the University of Wisconsin has devoted much time to a study of the matter. No, a rabbit's ears do more than just hear. They flatten out against said rabbit when it's very cold, thus to keep the beast warm. And they extend into the air when it's very hot, thus to radiate its excess body heat. How a rabbit handles its ears depends on the temperature, sort of.

If you're interested in knocking the transportation out from under 1,250,000 bacteria, swat a housefly. Such is said to be the average fly's germ count.

Count on a cow to eat about seven times as much as a sheep.

The temperature drops one degree for every 300-foot (90-m) rise in altitude.

Q. How long on the average are the ears and tail of the South American sloth?

A. Won't bite, sir. Has no tail or ears.

In the delightful tropics, you cannot hotfoot it out to pick lunch off a banana tree. Won't work. Even the bananas eaten there have to be picked green. Bugs and bacteria just flat out won't let them get ripe without rot.

Motion picture studies show fleas hop backwards, not forwards.

There is no wood in petrified wood. You want that explained? What once were woody cells long ago filled up with quartz. The wood itself disintegrated completely.

Q. How long are an elephant's eyelashes?

A. Four to 5 inches (10 to 12.5 cm).

Porpoises, too, have hair.

All I can tell you today about the spider is that it oils its legs so it won't get stuck in its web.

Likely you already know that a 1-inch- (2.5-cm-) thick rope of spider webbing is stronger than an inch-thick rope of iron.

Q. Do dogs eat toads?

A. Snap at them, yes. Eat them, no. Don't know how the toad does it, but it can make a dog let go instantly. And that dog will fuss and fume and shake its head for quite a while thereafter. Something emitted from the toad's skin, evidently.

Did you know that dahlias produce a sugar far superior either to cane or beet sugar?

There was a time when not just a few circus horses, but all well-trained riding horses, dropped to their knees—like camels—to receive their riders. That was before A.D. 420 when the stirrup was invented.

How long does it take an oyster to make a pearl? Depends. Average-sized pearl, about five years. Big pearl, figure 10 years. Those oysters aren't the food kind, please note. The dinner table oyster is prime at age 3.

Q. When does a cat purr, while exhaling or inhaling?

A. Both. One vocal cord purrs on the intake, the other on the outlet.

Gardenias give off a fancy fragrance. And so do orange blossoms. Put them together, though, and their fragrances cancel each other out.

SHARKS

Theorists once believed that sharks have to turn upside down to bite. That's not true, certainly. It is true, though, that sharks don't like to expose their heads or bodies above the water, and they probably wouldn't break the surface with their fins, either, if they weren't so stupid. Anyhow, that's 'why they do indeed turn upside down when they seize floating food. In the depths, they don't bother with such athletics.

All cats walk on their toes.

Q. Do dogs ever suffer from tonsillitis or appendicitis?

A. Tonsillitis, yes. Appendicitis, no. A dog doesn't have an appendix. Has something in just about the same place that looks like an appendix. It's called a caceum. But that bit of tissue evidently doesn't ever act up.

Q. At what age is the average dog full grown? Cat? Horse?

A. Dog, two years. Cat, one and a half years. Horse, four years.

CAT'S WHISKERS

Quick, how many rows of whiskers are on a cat's face? Say four, that's right. The longer whiskers are in the two middle rows. That cat has between 25 and 30 such whiskers, if average.

What good do these whiskers do for said cat, if anything? Theories abound. But one feline authority contends the whiskers let the cat know which direction the wind is coming from so the cat can track down any particular odor of interest.

Did you know why tree leaves work so well to muffle traffic noises? Because those leaves typically are just about the same lengths as the traffic sound waves.

MORE MAMMALS. The animal experts turn up just about 40 new species of mammals every year. And most of these previously undiscovered beasts are rodents. This comes up because a client wants to know how many kinds of rats there are. Nobody knows. Yet.

Q. How in the world do they salt peanuts without taking them out of their shells?

A. Nothing to it. They soak them in a 10-per cent salt brine before the roast.

It has long been said that low-flying swallows are a sign of impending bad weather. Quite so. Insects fly low in a humid atmosphere. The swallows swoop to the insects, that's all.

Natural vanilla flavoring comes from orchids.

Put all the fishes, reptiles, birds and mammals on one side of the scale. Put all the insects on the other side. Those insects would weigh more than three times as much.

In the intelligence ratings of animals, hogs rank ninth, sir.

PORCUPINES

A porcupine likes salt so much it'll eat just about anything containing same. Cite you this. A forest ranger left the window open on his parked car, and a porcupine ate the steering wheel. Everything except the spokes. Salt in the perspiration of the ranger's hands did that, obviously.

17 Law and Disorder

Murder is always a mistake; one should never do anything that one cannot talk about after dinner.

Oscar Wilde

How do you account for the fact that the average murderer—there is such a bird?—is about seven years six months younger than the victim?

Q. Can a 6-year-old child be punished by law for a crime?

A. By law, no. Or at least it's highly unlikely. Common law decrees nobody under age 7 is capable of criminal intent, so can't commit crimes.

Were you aware that the State of Virginia once levied a tax of $30 on every bathtub there?

Another reason you see so few drunken dogs in Chicago is the law there prohibits the feeding of whiskey to canines.

Say you're ferryboating across one of the Great Lakes. Do you consider yourself to be on the "high seas?" The U.S. Supreme Court says yes, you are.

Q. You know the caliber of most dueling pistols?

A. Anywhere from .50 to .75 (13 to 19 mm). Those were big-bore guns. The wounded pistol duelist who survived was the exception.

CRIME

The streets of most Latin American cities are safer than the streets of cities in the United States. But that doesn't go for Bogota, the pickpocket capital of the world. Also discount Caracas, where strong-arm robbery is common. And in Guatemala City, don't go out without your brother. A correspondent of lengthy experience thereabouts told me that.

Police scholars say the only thing obscene telephone callers have in common is they're almost never dangerous.

Note protesting students in Bombay, India, are demanding the right to cheat on their examinations. That's a bit much, Roger.

Just throw one little old beer can overboard in any harbor in Hawaii, and McGarrett could arrest you. That's outlawed.

It was in Rutledge, Vermont, where this judge asked the officer if he was absolutely certain the prisoner was drunk when arrested. Said the officer: "Your honor, I saw the fellow drop a penny in the parking meter, then look up at the courthouse clock, and holler that he had lost 12 pounds. What do you think?"

THE RIOT ACT

In 1714 during the reign of England's King George I, the British Parliament passed a lengthy law to curb public disturbances. Under it, if 12 or more persons were assembled illegally, disrupting the peace, a local official was required to read aloud to the gatherings the legislation in its entirety. It was from this, says our Language man, that we get the common phrase "reading The Riot Act," which was the name of that law.

Just about 300 people a year drop into New York City's Police Emergency Division to get tight rings sawed off their fingers.

If the New York City police can't get you for anything else, they might just jail you for opening an umbrella in the presence of a horse. That, too, is still outlawed there.

UNCORKER

Queen Elizabeth I of England appointed an official government "Uncorker of Ocean Bottles." Nobody else in the country was supposed to open bottles that drifted ashore there. A security matter, explained the Queen. British vessels sometimes sent her messages in floating bottles. Such as one that revealed how the Dutch overran a little island previously occupied by the Russians. That bottle message had been picked up by a fisherman on Dover Beach. The unscrupulous cad read it. The appointment of official Uncorker was continued for 230 years.

Pollsters say no professional is more likely to switch political parties from election to election than is the farmer.

When at church in Omaha, Nebraska, neither burp nor sneeze, please, such being illegal there.

LIGHT SWITCH

Where is the light switch to your bathroom? Inside the door or outside? Various building codes govern this matter differently in numerous municipalities. Some require it to be outside the door. On the theory you're less likely to have wet hands when you touch it there. Others require it inside. On the theory nobody but you should be able to turn it on or off when you're navigating around on slippery feet. A third group of city ordinance makers—bless them—regard the whereabouts of your bathroom switch as none of their business.

Q. What proportion of the shoplifters are kleptomaniacs?

A. One out of 100.

There are such things as mugger bees. Honey bees that send out raiding parties to attack other honey bees. Three or four of these muggers jump on a worker, beat him helpless, then steal his nectar. Hive law enforcement to protect the innocent and punish the guilty is said to be hopelessly inadequate.

ALIEN WHALES. Whale oil is taxed in the United States only if it's imported from a foreign country. That's what the tax court ruled. But whales don't live in foreign countries. That's what a whale catcher testified. The court thought it over, and said all right, from now on every whale takes the nationality of the flag that flies aboard the ship that catches it. So we have Norwegian whales, Russian whales, Japanese whales so on. Only whales that can be classified as world citizens any more are the whales that don't get caught.

Don't know exactly how many card cheaters there are in the U.S. but can report one company that sells marked cards grosses more than $1 million a year.

In Sweden, it's against the law to train a seal to balance a ball on its nose, bear in mind.

Q. Let's see if you can remember what type of business J. Edgar Hoover, back in 1941, accused of being "the new home of disease, bribery, corruption, crookedness, rape, white slavery, thievery and murder."

A. The motels.

BE SEATED. There was a time when the only people who sat in chairs were the people in positions of authority.

What's the first thing that all professional burglars do when they enter any sort of building? Figure the quickest way to get out. One of the same told me that.

Correspondents say it's still illegal in East Germany to take a picture of somebody waving goodbye from a train window. An anti-spy law.

Q. Why is a "straw vote" so called?

A. Comes from that ancient rural trick of throwing straws into the air to see which way the wind's blowing. Specifically, the politician known as Calico Charlie Foster, elected governor of Ohio almost 100 years ago, is thought to have been the first office seeker ever to take a straw vote.

A Virginia law requires all bathtubs to be kept out in the yards, not inside the houses.

An old California law makes a housewife liable to imprisonment if she doesn't boil her dustcloth.

Must mention, too, it's against the law to: 1. Doze off under a hair dryer in Florida. 2. Slap an old friend on the back in Georgia. 3. Play hopscotch on a Sunday afternoon in Missouri.

SPOONER. William Archibald Spooner, mentioned earlier, who so frequently got his tangue tongled, also once dismissed a college student with the following words: "You have deliberately tasted two worms and you can leave college by the town drain."

Studies in penitentiaries indicate that the criminal least likely to be tattooed is the convicted murderer. Tattoos were found most frequently on burglars. Then, on armed robbers. After that, in order, on rapists, kidnappers and would-be murderers.

Don't know who first said it, but increasingly of late you hear this quotation: "America is the only country in the world where they let the prisoners go home and lock up the jury."

Remember, too, it's against the law for two people to use the same finger bowl in Omaha.

Literal translation of one of the standard traffic signs in China reads: "Give large space to the festive dog that makes sport in the roadway."

After the law statisticians tallied up the facts about bad-check passers, they announced the typical paperhanger was 45 years old with a record of six years in jail.

LAWSUITS. Sir, have you as yet been involved in five major legal battles? If not, stand by. Law statisticians contend the average individual will be so involved during a lifetime. Those

152

predicted cases are: 1. Buyer versus seller. 2. Tenant versus landlord. 3. Driver versus driver. 4. Husband versus wife. 5. Insured versus insured company.

Please note, it was a Russian who devised that wise old proverb: "He who invokes the law takes a wolf by the ears."

MARKED CARDS. One out of every 10 card games for high stakes is played with marked cards. Do you find that hard to believe? Likewise. But it was the contention of an experienced witness at a U.S. Senate Committee hearing on gambling.

SCREAMERS. A manufacturer of burglary alarm systems says his studies show nothing works quite so well to scare off a culprit in the night as a woman's scream. He's auditioning screamers. And experimenting with tape recordings of same.

TRAVELLERS' CHECKS

The cunning thief who makes off with travellers' checks does not necessarily steal the whole book. Or so the detectives report. The experienced rapscallion "leafs" the book, instead. That is, he removes only several of the checks, stub and all, at random. Relatively few travellers ripped off ever realize it for some mysterious reason.

Am asked why juries usually are composed of 12 rather than any other number of persons. Goes way back. Court astrologers in ancient days appointed jury members. And selected each according to said juror's zodiac sign. On the theory that such would bring every type of mind possible to bear on the decision.

LIES. A trial lawyer of lengthy experience says, "You can't figure out when a man is lying unless you first figure out how he acts when he's leveling. This explains why lie detectors don't work on everybody. Some compulsive prevaricators

153

treat every word as a lie. Trouble with the lie detector, it's most effective where it's needed least, with the honest man."

Q. Which one of the United States has the least crime?

A. North Dakota.

That Latin word *candidus* meant "glittering white." Unblemished. Clean. Pure. It's where we got the word "candidates" for our public office seekers. More bitter observations coming up. Watch for same.

LEGAL TACTICS? No lawyer should forget that sage advice of old Cicero who said, "When you have no basis for an argument, abuse the plaintiff."

What's your favorite classified ad of all time? Mine is: "Lost and Found: To the party who shot the arrow into the air that fell to earth you know not where. I know where. Contact Rm. 701, County General Hosp."

Capital punishment is as bad a cure for crime as charity is for poverty.

Henry Ford

THE LAW. In Youngstown, Ohio, bear in mind it's illegal to ride on the roof of a taxicab. And it's against the law in Maine, you know, to walk down the street with your shoelaces untied.

Five banks a year on the average are shut down because of embezzlements.

Q. You know the purple ink that government inspectors stamp on meat? What's it made of?

A. Skins of dark grapes.

Q. Why are some prisons called penitentiaries?

A. Because the Quakers of Philadelphia who wanted them as a substitute for the death penalty thought the prisoners therein would be penitent. And in the first of such institutions, each prisoner was confined in solitary with the expectation that, unable to talk to any other prisoner for the term of the sentence, he would silently contemplate past crimes. It didn't work out precisely as planned.

In Iceland, anybody can practice medicine, providing said practitioner's shingle bears the title *Scottulaejnir*. Translates as "Quack Doctor."

GRAND THEFT

Remarkable the size of some things stolen! Somebody swiped an 80-foot bridge one night in Italy. Somebody else cut down and carted off an entire forest from a fairly sizable estate in Hungary. And I remember after World War II, French officials found on the bottom of an abandoned Navy dock a submarine which had been hijacked a couple of years earlier. Nobody knew by whom.

It's against the law in Kansas to eat rattlesnake meat in public.

Florida law forbids a housewife there to break more than three dishes a day.

Waterville, Maine, is that place where it's a violation to blow your nose in public.

And the most puzzling law of the bunch—sometimes I sit in front of the window trying to figure out the nature of the specific case that led to this judicial ruling—is the ordinance in Carmel, California, that makes it unlawful for a lady to take a bath in a business office.

18 Albanians Don't Get Headaches

HEADACHES. There's no word in the Albanian language that means "headache." Albanians don't get headaches. Seriously, that's the claim of a pharmacology researcher. Remarkable, if true. Can't really argue the matter, however. I don't get headaches either. Unless you want to count that dive years ago in the shallow end of the pool.

Those students of population growth who like the word "illegitimate" now report it's the appropriate term for 50 per cent of the children born in Brazil. They say it applies to slightly less than 15 per cent of U.S. babies.

BIG BUSINESS? The companies that employ four people or less in the U.S. outnumber the companies that employ 100 people or more by 23 to one.

FISH AND LEMON. Centuries ago it was believed—mistakenly, but believed nonetheless—that fish bones dissolved in lemon juice. That's what started the custom of serving lemon wedges with fish. Not for flavor's sake. But to dissolve the bones in the event a diner swallowed same.

GET IT RIGHT. Contrary to a previous report that the poinsettia is poisonous, several botanists who should know insist that's wrong, just a myth started long ago which nobody now dares to contradict.

Only one out of every 20 secretaries eats a full meal for lunch.

BULLFIGHTS. In the Philippines, the bulls fight each other, not people with weapons. Those bulls stand head to head, lock horns, and push. The loser is the bull that eventually gives up and runs away. The winner, if he's a winner often enough, is rewarded with a second career, that of a sire. Big thing in the Philippines, that bullfighting.

BOATS. It's just about 18 months after the man buys his first boat that he's most apt to decide to swap it in for a bigger boat. That's average. It's also just about 18 months after he buys his first boat that he's apt to give up boats altogether. Can go either way. A study of classified advertising customers indicates that.

Most popular color of contact lenses is blue.

What happens to school teachers who retire? They lose their principles. What happens to principals who retire? They lose their faculties. What, you've heard that?

PERSONAL SPACE

When you carry on an ordinary conversation with somebody, sir, how far away from said party do you like to stand? How close is too close to be comfortable? People differ greatly in this. A gentleman of science has noted: Every animal, including the human animal, lives within a personal space, surrounded by an imaginary circle. If you step into a stranger's own space, he is apt to get tense, possibly irritable, even hostile. Some theorists claim this explains why people who spend an inordinate amount of time in subways and elevators tend to be uncivil.

157

Do you know how rabbits talk to each other? By thumping their feet.

SCHOOL BUS. Am asked if the youngsters in the People's Republic of China go to school in buses. In pedicab buses, yes. A pedicap bus is a great big tricycle with the driver up front and behind him a completely enclosed cab in which the kids ride.

ORPHANS. In the speech of Tahiti, says our Language man, there is no word for "orphan." And there are no orphanages there. If youngsters lose their parents, those children are taken in immediately by another family. They are so uncivilized, those Tahitians.

Seven credit cards. That's how many the average citizen carts around now, according to the surveytakers.

No end to those old "signs by the side of the road," was there? Recall the one that goes: "This will never come to pass, a backseat driver out of gas."

158

Q. Doesn't that item of female apparel known as the falsie find a bigger market in the United States than in any other country?

A. A bigger market than in all other countries put together, in fact.

Q. Any slot machines in China?

A. There are. The Chinese call them "hungry tigers."

ARABS

Golda Meir once said she would know that true peace had arrived when she could go shopping in Cairo. Arab hospitality was different, though, a few generations ago. It required the head of an Arab family not only to welcome any visitor with food and a place to sleep, but to protect said party's life, even an enemy's, once that guest crossed the threshold.

In Helsinki, 10 times as many Finns speak Finnish as Swedish, even though Swedish is Finland's official second language. So the post office there is marked with a neon sign that reads the Finnish "Posti" for 10 seconds and the Swedish "Post" for one second alternately.

UPS AND DOWNS. Those marketing men who study the merchandising of everything report the sales of both tranquilizers and pep pills triple every year in the northerly Norwegian city of Tromso at the beginning of the two-month-long polar night. And during that darkness, the commitments to the mental hospital rise sharply, too.

Among names used in nursery rhymes, Jack is the most common. Remember that.

Why Africans who live in villages away from the big towns never get appendicitis is a mystery, but researchers there say such be the remarkable situation.

Company presidents have better vocabularies than professional writers. Professional writers have better vocabularies than college professors. Start again. Civil engineers have better vocabularies than accountants. Accountants have better vocabularies than musicians. And are you aware that musicians have better vocabularies than salesmen? That's the claim of our Language man after an extensive study of the pertinent surveys.

As to the world's champion coffee drinkers, list the Swedes. Import statistics prove that. The Danes, second. The Finns, third. The Norwegians, fourth. The U.S. citizenry? Eighth.

Q. What's so special about the soap that's called Castile?

A. Used to mean it was made with 100 per cent olive oil. That's how the Spaniards did it in ancient Castille. In recent years, though, a lot of soaps made with various other vegetable oils are labeled Castile.

Nowhere in his writings did William Shakespeare make mention of knives, forks or spoons. Why not? Because everybody, even the original Queen Elizabeth, ate with their fingers then, the savages.

TRAVEL. A New York City travel bureau printed on a Mexico City tour advertisement: "Don't drink the water." Irritated by this, a Mexico City travel bureau printed on a New York City tour advertisement: "Don't breathe the air."

OPTICAL ILLUSION. Flag of France has three vertical stripes. Blue, white and red. Said stripes are supposed to be of equal width. But they're not. Differences in the wavelengths of the colors make an optical illusion. So they'll seem equal, the stripes in the French flag have to be made in a proportion of 100 for the blue, 110 for the white and 124 for the red.

What one decoration can a doctor put in his waiting room that will be most soothing to his patients? That's what the medicos of Australia wanted to find out. So they commissioned a study. No, it wasn't a television set. According to the *Medical News Tribune,* one out of every three patients queried recommended a tankful of tropical fish.

SMILE. In Thailand, there still occasionally can be seen some elderly citizens whose front teeth are finely tattooed with the likenesses of Charlie Chaplin, Mickey Mouse and Dan Cupid. Such was a cosmetic custom there some years ago. Another fairly common tattoo for the four front teeth called for a spade, a heart, a diamond and a club.

Q. Says here an Iranian is not an Arab. Then what is an Arab?

A. Anybody whose mother tongue is Arabic. The Iranian speaks Persian.

EEL

Customary Christmas Eve dish in Italy is roast eel. Matter of fact, eel is pretty popular worldwide. The Japanese like it broiled on rice. Germans eat it smoked. Some Englanders jelly it. And there is a tradition among French gourmets that an eel must not be killed in any usual manner, but must be drowned in wine before it's cooked. That's humane.

Q. Is chess played in Japan?

A. It is. But with a different wrinkle. Captured pieces can be put back into service on any vacant square to fight for the capturing player.

TELL THE TRUTH

Do physicians tend to tell the truth? Most people think so, evidently. Psychologists at the University of Connecticut asked 400 citizens to rate the practitioners of 20 occupations as to their truthfulness. Doctors ranked No. 1. Used car salesmen, No. 20. The others: 2. Clergymen. 3. Dentists. 4. Judges. 5. Psychologists. 6. College professors. 7. Psychiatrists. 8. High school teachers. 9. Lawyers. 10. Law enforcement officials. 11. TV news reporters. 12. Plumbers. 13. Business executives. 14. U.S. Army generals. 15. TV repairmen. 16. Newspaper columnists. 17. Auto repairmen. 18. Labor union officials. 19. Politicians.

It's the reported contention of Los Angeles psychologist Paul Bindrim that public nudity will be condoned everywhere within the next 10 to 20 years. Please wait, Ethel.

That dessert preferred most by the Greenland Eskimos is watermelon imported from Israel.

That Chinese delicacy known as "100-Year-Old Eggs" actually are 100-day-old eggs, most usually. Client asks what they taste like. Beats me. Do know they're cured in a mixture of lime, salt and tea, plus. My mother, long gone these many years, was fairly knowledgeable about such gourmet goodies, and I recall she once said they taste like something you thought you'd thrown out.

Again am asked to identify the first vehicle ever used by man. No doubt about that. A floating log.

WESTERN GARB

It's true the high heels on western boots originally were designed to anchor the cowboy in his stirrups, but the height of the leather boots themselves was to protect him from burrs and snakes. No other footwear did the job so well. The broad-brimmed hat was a sunshine thing. Leather chaps on horseback fought the brambles and the cold wind. The neckerchief brought up to the nose blocked out the dust. Some citizens think these were affected costumes. They weren't. They fit the need.

Half of the world's Eskimos have never seen an igloo.

Q. Who are the men who stroke their beards when they meet instead of shaking hands or tipping hats?

A. The Turks of Sert. Strict Muhammadans, they. As soon as their whiskers start to grow, they shave their heads, but never again shave their faces.

CANINES. Note that a German-born dentist named Dr. Ursula Dietrich has invented a toothpaste for dogs called Doggy-Dent. The announcement preceded mild laughter here and there. Too bad. The citizenry ought not to be so skeptical. Remember, George Washington ordered his help to brush the teeth of his six white horses every morning. And it's widely known that monkeys not only brush their own teeth, but become expert with toothpicks.

The Russians are turning out antibiotics made from garlic.

HASTA LA VISTA. Customarily, when Mexicans wave goodby to you, they motion toward themselves, not toward you. Nice touch, that. They mean with those gestures that they want you to come back again.

KEEP YOUR SHIRT ON. Tokyo travel experts have published a booklet designed to educate Japanese air tourists on how to get along in the Western world. It advises them that they may in all good manners remove their jackets in front of other airplane passengers, but not their trousers.

Like oysters? How about squid? You too may be surprised to learn the squid eaters in this world outnumber the oyster eaters.

FINGER. Scholars recently returned from New Guinea said they noted a lot of elderly natives there had missing fingers. Research revealed that it was the custom some years ago for the young fighting man to give his lucky girlfriend a finger cut from the hand of an opponent. And said girlfriend wore that finger on a string around her neck.

Q. Those scientific sky watchers have designated radio waves from outer space with the term "LGM." What do the letters stand for?

A. Little Green Men.

Q. Does Santa Claus go to Japan?

A. Certainly, Virginia. They call him *Hoteiosho*.

CHRISTMAS STOCKINGS

Question arises as to how we came by that Christmas custom of hanging stockings by the fireplace. Originally, those socks were draped there to dry. Not every youngster had more than one pair, it should be noted. And presents were put in them overnight because that's where the presents were sure to be found in the morning.

If the Brazil nut comes from Bolivia, why do we call it the Brazil nut? Because it was shipped out by way of Brazil.

CROCODILES. Most of the people in India who are attacked by crocodiles are first bitten on the behind. Forgive that, please, but it's a fact. Why is interesting, if not fascinating. It remains a custom among numerous Indian women to stand hip deep in the water while they scrub their clothes on bank rocks.

GOURMET NOTES. Tea leaves originally were steamed, mashed into cakes, and eaten with salt, garlic and fat. In China's backwoods centuries ago—but not in China's front-woods—those cakes were used for money, too.

It's still the custom among most of the people in India to bathe only in moving water, never in a sit-down tub, which is regarded there as a filthy practice.

165

The old Greeks made napkins out of asbestos. Never washed them. Didn't have to. Just tossed them into the fire after the meal to burn them clean.

What, you can't name the only Arab nation without a desert? Try Lebanon.

That grass skirt isn't native to Hawaii, but to Samoa, sir.

Q. Who first said, "When in Rome, do as the Romans do?"

A. History records Saint Ambrose uttered such to Saint Augustine. Roman citizens fasted on Saturday. Milan citizens feasted on Saturday. To eat or not to eat, that was the query Saint Augustine put to Saint Ambrose who then delivered his most famous one-liner.

Most people put the telephone to the left ear. Possibly because of the habit of taking notes with the right hand, I don't know. It's a fact, however, that most people hear better with the right ear. Far more often than otherwise do mechanics cock their right ears toward the engines when listening to oddball noises.

It's estimated that one out of every 20 citizens nationwide is some kind of vegetarian.

Clasp your hands directly in front of your face. Your right thumb, not your left thumb, is the closer to your chin, no? Such is how the enormous majority clasps the hands. Not just the enormous majority of right-handers, but of left-handers, too.

NETS. It's a matter of record that some natives of South Pacific islands bend bamboo into six-foot (1.8-m) hoops, wait for the giant spiders thereabouts to weave their webs across same, then use those webs most effectively as fishnets.

166

You've heard about that professional perfume tester known in the trade as a "nose." To merit recognition as a great nose, said sniffer must be able to waft the scent in the oil from a single rose petal and figure out whether or not it would do well in a specific perfume formula.

What do modern forks and modern shoes have in common? Design of both is about 175 years old. Before 1800 in this country, there were no four-tined forks in common use nor were there any separate shoes for right and left feet.

Was the ancient Egyptians in about 3000 B.C. who first embalmed their dead citizens. They also embalmed their dead crocodiles.

Did you know that both chili con carne and hot tamales are not Mexican dishes? Both were created in southern Texas.

It's also a matter of record that the cannibals of the Marquesas Islands long regarded the female forearm as the choicest morsel of human flesh.

Twice as many whites as blacks are color blind, proportionately. And twice as many blacks as American Indians are color blind, proportionately. And twice as many American Indians as Eskimos are color blind, proportionately.

Q. Is there any country in the world where all the grownups, I mean absolutely all of them, can read and write?

A. Only Iceland as far as I know.

It was in the year 1659 that Massachusetts outlawed Christmas, incredibly enough. Yes, sir, the law stipulated "that anybody found observing Christmas in any way" was to be fined five shillings.

19 What Are We Doing Here?

Every year it takes less time to fly across the Atlantic and more time to drive to the office.

American Mercury

Sixty-four inmates in the Berkshire County Jail in Massachusetts went on a hunger strike. Their complaints: The food was abominable and they were not allowed to have seconds.

The plastic surgeons in Los Angeles now report that men with concave chests are getting breast implants.

Why I do not know, but an East German inventor has devised a machine to milk mice.

Already told you our Language man is collecting reconditioned proverbs. Credit L. Gibbs of Stillwater, Oklahoma, with these: "A stitch in time holds the magazine together." "Hot the rod and spoil the child." "A bird in the hand makes it hard to blow your nose."

BOREDOM TEST

Take a pencil and a tablet, check the time exactly, and start drawing X's and O's. Come on, keep at it. How long can you continue this fascinating pastime before you give up and throw down your pencil? The average college student in a series of such tests stuck it out 17 minutes. The average elementary student quit after nine minutes. Just tried it myself and hung in there for about 30 seconds. Some University of California scholars contend the longer you can last in this boredom test, the more contented you'll be over the years.

Q. Is there any one weeknight in particular when the most people commit suicide?

A. Can only report the statistics out of the Los Angeles Suicide Prevention Center. Wednesday is the peak night there, it's said.

ANTI-THEFT DEVICE. Writes a cunning client: "Seven years ago, my wife's car was ransacked. Of about $500 worth of Christmas presents. Since, at my direction, she has kept a life-sized baby doll, wrapped in receiving blankets, in a crib basket in the back seat. Thieves won't monkey around in a car with a baby in it. It works. She never even bothers to lock it anymore."

Don't care if it is the most profitable grub on the market, I certainly wouldn't eat it. Dog food. Do you realize the citizenry spends almost four times as much on it as on baby food?

Young men and girls between ages 16 and 19 tend to abandon their reasoning powers in romantic attachments no matter how good the judgment might be in other matters. This odd loss of common sense sometimes occurs again between the ages of 39 and 45. And it's likely to crop up once more in the late 60s among those whom deaths leave in solitude. Such is the contention of a renowned expert on matrimony. Our Love and War man confirms the finding. But he cannot explain why clear-thinking people suddenly develop blind spots about affection.

169

WITCHES. When a witch was sent to the stake, her cats were burned along with her. In 1484, that was. Pope Innocent VIII so ordained it.

HARD TO GET

That party who plays hard to get tends to inspire more passion in the person who is trying to do the getting. And the romantic pushover inspires less amorous interest. This matter of common knowledge has been confirmed by our Love and War man after extensive study. He is in agreement on it with such great love and war experts as Socrates, Ovid, Terence and the Kamasutra.

HANGOVER CURE. They put a slice of salami over a jigger of vodka and then sip the vodka through the salami. That's how the Hungarians fight a hangover.

In death and destruction, World War I was seven times as large as the 901 other major wars that occurred before it since 500 B.C. And World War II was about four times as large as World War I. Or so the historians contend.

PROPER JOB CLUB. Of San Diego, California, Mr. Sprinkle, a lawn-care specialist. Of Bozeman, Montana, Mr. Grabb, Montana State University football team pass receiver. Of Lebanon, Pennsylvania, Dr. Fix, authority on drug abuse.

No doubt you've been through that little piece of comic business wherein you and somebody else meet on the sidewalk and both feint to the right and the left to avoid bumping. What causes this is the locking of eyes. Peculiarly, research reveals, if you don't look into the oncoming faces, it never happens.

COURTING. A lover on the island of Trobriand customarily bites off his ladyfriend's eyelashes. He would never take her out to dinner, however, unless they were married. To share a meal with her would disgrace her. A terrible offense.

Like molesting. Or indecent exposure. Or statutory assault. That unspeakable.

Did Nazi Fuhrer Adolf Hitler ever really own land in Colorado? So it was reported in 1942. By none other than the then mayor of Kit Carson, Colorado, in fact. The 8,960 acres (3,584 hectares) supposedly inherited by Hitler from relatives in Germany, was four miles (6.4 km) from Kit Carson, and neighboring ranchers grazed their stock on it.

WORRY

Am now able to report what sort of college student worries the most. It's the psych major. Second on the list of worriers is in home economics. Third, in business. Fourth, education. And fifth, engineering. Or such be the findings in a study of 1,600 upperclassmen. The scholar who undertook this research is worried, too. That most of the upcoming psychologists will be chronic handwringers.

It is also true that a fifth of the citizenry accounts for four-fifths of the serious accidents.

LAUGHS. A student of the mind contends the jokes at which you laugh the loudest show the way you'd really like to behave, if your conscience wouldn't stand in your way.

Q. How often does the calendar repeat itself?

A. Every six years, 11 years, 11 years, six years, 11 years, 11 years, six years, 11 years, 11 years, six years, and so on. Excuse the poetry, don't know how else to state it.

You've heard of those people referred to as larks, who leap up early, and those called owls, who stay up late. Another way in which they differ, it's said, is larks almost always like hearty breakfasts. Owls rarely eat breakfasts at all.

Among those successful gentlemen who earn more than $100,000 a year, surveys show, 14 per cent never eat any breakfast.

Wake up an elephant with a bang and said animal is apt to be cross all day. Circus men know that. They're exceedingly gentle in the way they awaken those big beasts.

MOUSTACHE

The moustache in England 150 years ago was the privilege only of classy fellows. Working men were not sanctioned to wear same. And when the tradespeople defied convention to grow moustaches, the British aristocracy came unglued. Spokesmen for it said the popularization of the moustache was a profound threat to the national institutions. Do you ever get the feeling that we're all nuts? Wacky? Battier than billygoats? And always have been? Ever since the beginning? I do.

172

That Peter Minuit bought Manhattan Island for $24 is widely known. But did you know he was fined by the Dutch for extravagance?

Hottest months at the Equator are March and September.

Surveys show 12 per cent of Americans would settle in some other country, if they could afford it.

DATELINE

The international dateline falls directly across the island of Taveuni in Fiji. A storekeeper there put up a shop astraddle that line with doors on both sides of it. Thus, he beats the Sunday closing law. He can run back and forth between Friday and Saturday several times a minute. And if he so chooses, he can skip Monday altogether. Great!

Not many citizens realize the Statue of Liberty originally was to be set up at the Suez Canal.

Among inventions registered at the U.S. Patent Office is a cigarette package that coughs.

During any given year you can figure that about 44 per cent of all murders are done with handguns, 7 per cent with rifles, 9 per cent with shotguns and 23 per cent with knives. Blame hammers, axes, baseball bats, broken bottles—whatever—for the remaining 17 per cent.

LIGHTNING

Only one out of 10 souls killed by lightning gets hit in the morning. It's an afternoon tragedy, usually.

It's not unusual for a lightning bolt to deliver 25,000 times more current than was customarily shot through the electric chair for an execution.

CANINE COIF. There's a London hairdresser named Signor Diagio who makes a tidy income by creating identical hairpieces for the lady customer and her dog.

Q. Name the world's oldest continuously occupied metropolis.

A. That would be Istanbul. From whence cometh the tulip, the table fork and the Turkish bath.

"Education is the process, not the destination, the process of moving from cocksure ignorance to thoughtful uncertainty." T. H. Bell, U.S. Commissioner of Education, said that.

The new seagoing supertankers are so long that a lot of the seamen who sleep in the stern but work up forward ride to their jobs every day on bicycles.

Should cows wear bras? Hold on, maybe that's not such a ridiculous query. An outfit called the Franksville Specialty Company recently started to manufacture bras for dairy stock. It's not a moral matter. Idea is to keep milk production high by preventing injuries to udders.

TIME

How many hours a week do you spend with your family? Wait, don't count sleeping. I mean working, playing, talking. Students at the University of California, Santa Barbara, checked this out to find an average. Four hours a week is all, they contend.

Parents talk with their youngsters only about 20 minutes a week on the average. That's the claim of a University of Wisconsin researcher. By "talk to," this authority means even the take-out-the-garbage orders and the may-I-go-downtown queries.

Quarrel not at all. No man resolved to make the most of himself can spare the time for personal contentions. Better give your pants to a dog than be bitten by him.

Abe Lincoln

JOBS

What's the most boring job in the world? That's what researchers at Harvard's Institute for Policy Studies wanted to know. Their intensive investigations resulted in a list of these five jobs as the most boring of all: 1. Assembly line worker. 2. Elevator operator. 3. Pool typist. 4. Bank guard. 5. Housewife. Also listed by this outfit as among the most boring of occupations are those of key puncher, copy machine operator and highway toll collector.

WHEN TO QUIT

Recommendation No. 2 on William P. Lear, Sr.'s list of six suggestions on how to become successful reads: "Learn when

175

to quit a job. As soon as you've learned how to do your job as well as it can be done, ask for more responsibility in your company or a different job. If you don't get it, get out."

STUTTERING

A voice specialist says that stutterers don't stutter when they whisper. This is the same authority who contends that northern stutterers can get rid of the impediment if they affect a southern drawl, and that southern stutterers can do likewise if they affect a New England twang. Interesting, if true.

One person out of every 100 stutters.

A lawyer in Indianapolis, Indiana, sometime back asked a criminal court judge there to permit an examination by a psychiatrist of the jury members in a robbery case. Request denied, said the judge, there's no statutory requirement that a juror be sane.

There's a plastic surgeon in New York City who makes most of his money by cutting dimples into cheeks and chins.

It is now possible to buy in some gourmet shops spiced muskrat meat in gelatin.

FOR THE MAN WHO HAS EVERYTHING

The marketing boys say they soon expect to sell cufflinks made of petrified dinosaur dung.

An ordinance in Brewton, Alabama, specifically requires all people on city streets there either to walk or to ride. Imagine it's aimed at preventing them from sleeping, crawling or just standing around, don't know.

Was a time when it was against the law in Cambodia to insult a rice plant.

Do you know any man who wears false eyelashes? Neither do I. But the marketers of such lashes say 50 million pairs a year are sold. And they swear numerous men wear same.

A billboard in that carrot country around Holtville, California, advertises a pesticide thusly: "Fear no Weevil."

The McDonald's fast food chain uses up more beef per year than any one of most of the countries in Africa, I'm told.

A bookstore owner in Raleigh, North Carolina, contends that volume most often stolen year after year is the Bible. Incredible!

20 The Hard Facts

Nothing is so fallacious as facts, except figures.

George Canning

Are you old enough to remember when a Santa Claus costume was not thought to be authentic unless it was decorated with yak hair?

Both flies and frogs have been known to catch athlete's foot.

FIRST AID

Say you arrive at the scene of a car wreck where you find somebody who not only suffers a terrible open wound on a leg but also appears no longer to be breathing. What do you do first, apply a tourniquet or start artificial respiration? No. 1 on the first aid chart here is stop the bleeding. A soul so injured can survive the lack of oxygen longer than the extreme loss of blood. This medical consultation is offered without charge. Expect no bill.

Statistically, you're 14 times less likely to survive a boating accident than a highway smashup.

More people who don't work hard commit suicide than people who do work hard.

In William Shakespeare's day, so many babies failed to survive their first two years that the average age of death among humans overall was somewhere near six years, the dismal record shows.

The backseats in a car are three times as safe as the front seats, statistically.

Q. What happened to P. T. Barnum's elephant Jumbo?

A. Died in a train wreck. Jumbo's skeleton, except for a missing toe, is at the Museum of Natural History in New York. That toe, please note, wound up in the possession of an Ontario businessman, E. H. Flach, who turned it into an ink well.

Q. Do you know how to tell you're too fat?

A. Sure, you say, "I'm too fat." Wait, that's flip. The experts contend you can be sure you're overweight if, when you pinch the skin on your midsection, more than half an inch separates your finger and thumb.

Nowhere in the Bible does it either number or name the wise men in the nativity story.

Early makers of playing cards in Great Britain did not print ace of spades for each deck. The British government printed aces of spades. And the card manufacturers only acquired them when they paid their taxes on the decks. That's why that dandy big design even on today's aces of spades differs from the designs on the other aces.

Diamond dust is black.

SICK

Doesn't follow that the youngster who is sick a lot in childhood will be sick a lot when grown up. Nor will a sturdy steady child necessarily be sturdy and steady when an adult. Scholars studied several thousand telephone company employees. About 30 per cent of them accounted for 80 per cent of all the time lost because of ailments. And their records indicated most of them weren't particularly susceptible to sickness when younger. Conclusion was the majority didn't like their marriages or didn't like their jobs or both. That was what got them down.

HITCHHIKERS. Arizona police checked out 100 hitchhikers. Over a period of time. Along one stretch of road. Consider this: Exactly 84 had criminal records. And 12 either were adolescent runaways or servicemen away without official leave. That left four, just four, who hadn't been crossways with the law, or were about to be.

Q. Which one of the United States gets the least sunshine?

A. Alaska. Sun shines there about 31 per cent of the time.

BANANA PEEL. The latest debunking of cartoonists' notions was revealed in a recent study of the files in hospital emergency rooms. Not one victim of a fall reported having slipped on a banana peel.

PRIMES. When is the prime of life? Depends on the beast. Among men, it's said, the physical prime is in the early 20s, the mental prime in the early 50s. Among herring, the prime is about at age 10. That's not physical or mental, it's gastronomical. They taste best then. A Norwegian told me that.

Poison oak isn't oak and poison ivy isn't ivy.

Researchers say their studies indicate 22 out of every 25 people of Caucasian heritage put on their right shoe first.

The bald eagle is larger at age 2 than at age 4. Can you explain why? Neither can I.

WHITE EYES. Those movie script writers who've had their Apache Indian characters refer to white men as "white eyes" got it right. In Geronimo's time, that was the standard Apache nomenclature for the whites.

By the time they're 25, half the men in this country are married. The same can be said for only a quarter of the men in Europe.

The wheels on a supermarket shopping cart typically get replaced three times before the thing is junked after 10 years.

A barber, dentist and foot doctor all in one was that practitioner of the first century. This is to say the same specialist took care of hair, teeth and corns. And there's no record that said party washed hands between patients, might mention.

Chances are your left foot is just a little bit larger than your right. So say the shoemakers. And it doesn't matter whether you're left-handed or right-handed.

Statistically, it's far more likely a golfer will be struck by lightning than a swimmer will be attacked by sharks.

SEE YOUR DENTIST. Ask 100 people how often they visit their dentists and 88 will say once a year. However, the dental records show only 40 really do.

WEDDINGS

Will bet you a small unspecified sum that no matter how many church weddings you've attended, you've never seen a bride walk down the aisle. The aisles in a church are the walkways that go lengthwise down both sides, and they're separated from the main by pillars. What the bride walks down is the nave.

How long does it take to plan the perfect formal church wedding? At least three months, the experts aver. Details, details.

Never buy a used car in the rain. So advises a retired seller of same. Rain hides bad paint jobs and bad body work, he says. It also muffles engine irregularities and discourages an adequate road test. Be advised.

THE COMMON COLD. University of Virginia researchers now claim more common colds are passed by handshakes than by coughs and sneezes.

Q. What's the best guess of the scholars as to the life span of the average prehistoric man?

A. About 18 years is the most common estimate.

If everybody in this world who doesn't have a home were to walk single file in front of you, the parade would last about two years.

EINSTEIN. It has been reported by reliable sources that the great Albert Einstein during his many years at Princeton never wore socks.

Research indicates mosquitoes do indeed tend to bite somebody who's recently eaten a banana.

The dirtiest skin surface on the body is the face.

The average person in a course of a lifetime walks a distance equivalent to almost three times around the equator.

JELLYFISH. Remember, even a dried out jellyfish dead for months can sting you badly if you walk over it with bare feet.

Most mental patients don't have violent seizures, quite true. But those who do tend to suffer same, in too many instances to be coincidental, between 3 and 4 a.m. Or so a medical specialist tells me. Why is a mystery.

Exceptions abound, certainly, but studies now indicate that the son of a full-blown alcoholic tends either to turn into an alcoholic himself or a teetotaler, but not usually a moderate imbiber.

No medical specialist is more likely to develop back trouble than is the psychiatrist.

Q. Give me the mental age of a moron.

A. Between eight and twelve years, technically.

It takes 1.53 acres (0.61 hectares) of cultivated land a year to feed a person who eats meat, but it only takes half an acre (0.2 hectare) to feed a vegetarian.

In its entirety, that poem by Ruth S. Schenley reads: "Little snax, bigger slax."

WORKING MOTHERS

What the scholars up in Michigan wanted to find out recently was how well mothers and dads seemed to be getting along with their teenage children. They checked out 2,000 youngsters. And they concluded that the most harmonious adolescent-parent relationships occurred in families in which the mothers worked somewhere for wages up to 32 hours each week.

GLASS. The longer glass stays under water, the stronger it gets. The naval researchers say nothing else is like that, nothing.

If you're about to buy a used car, look at the brake pedal. It can't tell you how far the car has traveled, but it will indicate whether the previous owner was a gentle driver or a hot-foot highballer. Greater the wear on that pedal, higher the repair bills, usually. Such is the claim of a mechanical expert.

One traffic accident every 10 years, that's what the typical driver can expect if the law of averages holds up. And a ticket every 9.2 years.

Emergency room statistics indicate the time of day you're most likely to crash into a glass door is the late afternoon.

To his list of reconditioned proverbs, our Language man has added: "If at first you don't succeed, read the directions, dummy!"

184

21 For Better or Worse

When I was a young man, I vowed never to marry until I found the ideal woman. Well, I found her. But, alas, she was waiting for the ideal man.

Robert Schuman

Q. Which state of the U.S. has the lowest marriage age?

A. That would be New Hampshire. A 14-year-old boy can marry a 13-year-old girl there, if the folks and court okay it.

Among the most happily married citizens, one matrimonial study shows, are the mathematics teachers.

Am asked why matrimonial partners never walk side by side in New Guinea. Any display of affection is frowned upon there. That's why. To be seen kissing or holding hands, of course, would be an outrage. But even a stroll together down the jungle trail would be too apt to betray some feelings of fondness.

Young fellow, if you're 19, the statistical odds are you've already met the girl you're going to marry, even though the probabilities indicate you've not yet proposed. This does not mean you're now certain which of your feminine acquaintances you'll eventually marry. It's also a statistical fact that most of the married were not the first choices of their matrimonial mates.

CHOOSING A PARTNER

There's a curious difference in the ways that single girls and bachelors pick their romantic partners. The girl might have a dozen boyfriends, none of whom seems to be like another or anything like the sort of fellow she eventually winds up marrying. But the young bachelor is inclined to select all his ladyfriends, including finally his wife, for their similar qualities.

Those family tree experts think there are about 3.5 million people nationwide directly descended from John Alden and Priscilla of Mayflower fame. That romantic pair had 11 children. Who in turn. And who in turn.

Every tenth homicide in this country involves a husband and wife.

NEWLYWEDS

What were the 10 most important items in your budget when you got married? The matrimonial counselors say the following are rated as such: Bedroom furniture, linens, living room furniture, refrigerator, automobile, washing machine, dinette set, television, radio and rugs. Their findings came from a survey of a sizable sampling of brides. Exactly 94 per cent of those girls listed bedroom furniture as indispensable. The remaining 6 per cent did not.

Research at Columbia University suggests that approximately 50 per cent of all family fights start in the hour before dinner.

BIGAMIST. Was the great Fred Allen who defined a bigamist as "the chap who has had one too many."

A family is a unit composed not only of children, but of men, women, an occasional animal and the common cold.

Ogden Nash

Q. Where does "overindulging the children" rate on that famous list of the seven money traps in matrimony?

A. It's No. 6. No. 1 is the urge to splurge. No. 2, too much house. No. 3, too much car. No. 4, a hobby that keeps getting bigger. No. 5, a company expense account. No. 7, clothing.

MORE ON CHOOSING A MATE

It's commonly believed a man picks out a wife who reminds him of his mother while a woman picks out a husband who reminds her of her father. But that's not right. Recent research indicates both the man and the woman are most influenced in their selections of matrimonial mates by their mothers. If a woman regards her mother as stern, she's likely to go for a stern husband. If she thinks of her mother as gentle, she looks for a gentle husband. The father of the bride or groom just doesn't have all that much to do with it, poor fellow.

MOST WONDERFUL MAN IN THE WORLD

A doctor of renown contends that the woman who describes her husband as "the most wonderful man in the world" probably needs psychiatric treatment. He is not just being sardonic. He says that wifely comment is a serious tipoff to emotional sickness. Our Love and War man is looking for another doctor of renown.

It's reported that more than 10,000 marriages a year now are directly traceable to romances which begin during coffee breaks.

This week's preferred classified ad reads as follows: "The Parents of Newborn Babies Club will hold its weekly meeting Saturday at 4 a.m."

MARRIAGE IS . . .

Danny Thomas said, "Anyone who thinks marriage is a fifty-fifty proposition doesn't understand women or fractions." Montaigne said, "Marriage is a cage. The birds without try desperately to get in, and those within try desperately to get out." The *Irish Independent* said, "Marriage is like a violin. After the beautiful music is over, the strings are still attached." And Oscar Levant said, "Marriage is a triumph of habit over hate." Interesting. But too cynical. Still say Harold Orben's contention was better. He claimed marriage is a sociological system of producing motors for tricycles.

DECISIONS

When it's the husband but not the wife who earns the family income, it's usually the husband but not the wife who makes the big decisions. A client asks if the reverse is true when the wife but not the husband earns the family income. No, oddly enough. Scholars with the Florida State Research Council studied the matter. And they contend the husband has considerably more voice in family decisions when his wife is the breadwinner than when she isn't. Why is a mystery. Maybe it's because the wife is too tired at night to argue.

A gambling man who knows his odds should bet you 2,600 to one you did not elope when you got married.

BRIDAL VEIL. That piece of netting known as the bridal veil has its history, too. Started out as a sack over her head, be it known. Those old boys carted off those old girls in rather an abrupt manner sometimes.

The Roman emperor Justinian permitted divorce by mutual consent, providing that both the separating husband and wife vowed lifelong chastity thereafter. In the lingo of Burt Reynolds, he must have been out of his bird, old Justinian.

Girls tend to be more dedicated than boys to the notion of getting married as soon as possible. Peculiarly, though, wives are not as apt to be as content as husbands with their state of wedlock once the thing is done. When the researchers went to work on this topic, they learned that a fairly large proportion of bachelors enjoyed the belief that they could get along in a dandy manner without marriage. Far fewer single girls thought likewise. But in the followup, more wives than husbands were sorry they married. And the divorced women who said they were through with matrimony far outnumbered the divorced men who felt the same.

One hundred years ago in what's now Ethiopia, it was the custom for a husband and wife to sleep in a single nightgown.

LOVERS FIGHT

Lots of couples who love each other deeply divorce because they can't stand their fights. They marry new partners. But somehow they keep in touch. To go on fighting. About support payments, visitation rights, lawyers' fees, unpaid bills, whatever. They make issues to quarrel over. For the rest of their lives, if possible. A matrimonial expert of some renown claims such former lovers are permanently hooked on each other. Far more so than on the lukewarm mates they marry later. But they just don't know how to handle such fierce affection, sad to report. Our Love and War man says that's interesting, and turns the page.

The clothes a wife wore on any given day weighed about a fourth as much as the clothes her husband wore. That was before the feminine pantsuit came along. Her clothes now weigh about half as much as his.

PRICE OF A BRIDE

Client asks if brides are still for sale in the South Pacific. In New Guinea, they are. At least in the remoter highlands. Price varies, depending on the bride's experience or lack of same. An inexperienced bride is said to sell for about $250, five pigs and one cassowary bird. But a bride married once earlier is only valued at $35 and one cassowary. That's ap-

189

proximate. Understand a lot of dickering goes on in these transactions.

Price of a new bride in Jamestown when the English first settled there was 120 pounds (54 kg) of tobacco.

Q. What's a librocubicularist?

A. Someone who reads in bed.

ZULU MARRIAGE

Here's how these marriage matters work among the Zulu in the Republic of South Africa: The husband lives with his No. 1 ladyfriend in the big house. In a hut to the left of the big house lives his No. 2 ladyfriend. She's called his left-hand wife. In a hut to the right of the big house lives his No. 3 ladyfriend. And she's called his right-hand wife. Sons of No. 1 inherit. But if No. 1 has none, sons of No. 3 inherit. Sons of No. 2 don't count.

Do you know what the primary ambition of a Zulu's wife is? To help her husband acquire sufficient means to buy another wife. So they can split the chores.

How could I have neglected so long to tell you this week's favorite classified ad? It reads: "Personals: Dear Raggedy Ann, this is goodbye. I've fallen in love with a Barbie doll. (Signed) Raggedy Andy."

ENGAGEMENTS. Only 14 per cent of the nation's brides are engaged to the men they actually marry more than one year. Length of the average engagement is six months. Our Love and War man says that is as it should be. Engagements that are considerably shorter or considerably longer tend to raise the odds against happy matrimony.

TWINS. If a woman had twins, she automatically was accused of infidelity. Anthropologists say that was the situation in numerous ancient societies. There were pockets of ignorance worldwide wherein it was thought that no woman could have two babies at the same time by one father.

If you want to make sure that one of your offspring is a genius, father at least 200 of same. Statistically, there's at least one genius among that many youngsters, the researchers contend.

EASY DIVORCE. In the Balanta tribe of Africa, a bride remained married until her wedding gown was worn out. If she wanted a divorce after two weeks, all she had to do was rip up her dress. This was the custom until about 20 years ago, anyway.

Young lady, can you see yourself wearing a wig with tresses eight feet long? Such there be. In Copenhagen, Denmark. Brides rent it for weddings.

Was the custom in old Bulgaria for the bride and groom to play tug-of-war after the wedding ceremony with a loaf of bread. Whoever broke off the bigger piece was supposed to become boss of the house.

Moral indignation is jealousy with a halo.

H. G. Wells

INCEST. A brother and sister married each other. Among their children, a brother and sister married. Among theirs, another brother and sister married. This sort of thing was a common practice in a lot of societies years ago. Cleopatra, for instance, was the offspring of six generations of incest.

Married men tend to be better drivers than single men. Not just safer. Better. No, I didn't say that. An Iowa State College scholar so proclaimed after a study of 1,000 drivers.

FOREVER SINGLE

Certain statisticians claim that any man who hasn't been married by the time he's 36 is a confirmed bachelor. But they only allow a woman to grow to age 31 before they label her a spinster. Is that equitable?

Was not so many years ago in Thailand that any girl who was still unmarried at age 30 had the right to apply to the government for a husband.

SADIE HAWKINS. It's reported by the matrimonial experts that 90 per cent of the marriages in which the women have done the proposing have been successful.

Under the law in Whitesville, Delaware, a girl who proposes matrimony to a man commits that offense called "disorderly conduct."

KISS HER GOODBYE

The matrimonial pollsters contend their studies indicate the man who kisses his wife goodbye when he leaves for work every morning averages a higher income than does the fellow who doesn't do that thing. Husbands who exercise the rituals of affection tend to be more painstaking, more stable, more methodical, thus higher earners, it's believed. Our Love and War man says it's understandable. To him maybe.

HAPPINESS. Husbands are happier than single women. Single women are happier than married women. Married women are happier than bachelors. Or so say University of Chicago scholars.

MARITAL TENSION. The great psychologist Carl Jung claimed, "The most surprising element necessary to make a happy marriage is tension. Look at this in terms of everyday life. Is a conversation likely to be interesting if you know beforehand that your partner will agree with everything you say? Mentally, morally and physically, nature has created extreme differences between man and woman, so that he finds his opposite in her and she in him. This creates tension." Remember that. For happiness' sake, drum up a white-knuckle debate with your matrimonial mate.

AMISH MARRIAGE

"A plump wife and a big barn never did any man harm." That's a popular saying among the Amish of Pennsylvania.

The ceremony to marry an Amish couple traditionally takes about 3 hours 30 minutes.

"A courting mirror" is what it was called. Generations ago. When a bashful fellow wanted to propose matrimony, he'd look into said mirror, theoretically leaving his reflection therein, then hand same to his girl. If she looked thereupon, that meant yes. But if she turned the mirror face down, that signified no. The language boys insist this novel bit of stage business is where we first got the phrase "to turn him down."

He was a thrice-married attorney in Illinois. And when he died, in accordance with the instructions in his Last Will and Testament, his tombstone listed the names of his three wives followed by the simple sentence: "The defense rests."

BETTY CROCKER

Longing for a ladyfriend who knows how to cook, many is the single fellow who has mailed a matrimonial proposal to Betty Crocker. Unfortunately, there is no Betty Crocker. Never was, either. An ad man dreamed up that fictional female. Picked Betty because it's a popular name. And Crocker after the much-admired William G. Crocker, a one-time director of General Mills. Whose face it is that portrays Betty Crocker I don't know. Will check further.

This ad turned up in the courtship column of an English newspaper's classified section: "Gentleman owning a tractor wishes to correspond with lady owning a thresher. Please send picture of the thresher."

Sign sighted in a Kentucky restaurant: "Marriage has three rings: Engagement ring, wedding ring and suffering." Too cynical, says our Love and War man.

Why do you suppose the city fathers of Hartford, Connecticut, once passed an ordinance to make it illegal to kiss your wife on Sunday there?

194

NOT-SO-EASY DIVORCE. Divorce is a pretty rough experience, but it's not as rough now as once it was in Moldavia. That was a principality of what today is a part of Rumania. There was no alimony, no support payment, no separate maintenance, no legal fee and no court cost. Alexandru Lapuseanu, the ruler of the place from 1546 to 1568, simplified the situation greatly. He just imposed the death penalty on anybody who even started divorce proceedings.

COLD FEET. Most recent research indicates just about 9,000 romantic couples each year take out marriage licenses, then fail to use them.

She described her husband as "a bore," did this San Antonio wife who filed for divorce. "Just what is a bore?" inquired the judge. She thought about it, then quoted, "A person who deprives you of solitude without providing you with company." The record shows the judge regarded that as grounds sufficient.

Men marry because they are tired, women because they are curious: Both are disappointed.

Oscar Wilde

22   Lions Are Lousy Parents and Penguins Are Stupid

Lions are lousy parents. They beat up their cubs, frequently fatally. That has been proved.

A penguin is stupid. Toss a live fish on the ground and the bird won't even recognize it as food. Yet wiggly fishes, plucked out of the water, are just about all a penguin eats.

Q. Do giraffes kick each other?

A. Each other, no. They kick lions. When they fight each other, they stand side by side and take turns swinging their necks. Object of the swinger is to hit the swingee anywhere between the shoulder and ear. Object of the swingee is to duck.

DOG CITY

Rome now has more homeless cats per square mile than any other city in the world, it's said. Interesting. Time was though, when Rome was the dog haven of the world. The most common Latin sign in ancient Rome was *Cave Canem* meaning "Beware of Dog." Imperial law then required every watchdog owner to post such a warning. That dog was a status symbol. It told the citizenry thereabouts that the master of the beast owned property valuable enough to be worth guarding.

Not much sounds as lonely as the howl of a wolf. And that is as it should be. It has now been determined by the natural scientists that loneliness is what prompts a wolf to howl, most usually. That's its way of finding the other wolves when it gets separated from the pack.

HANDSHAKE. Among the tritest of trivia is the old report that the handshake originated among medieval men who sought to prove they carried no weapons. Maybe so, maybe so. Still, chimpanzees in the wild have been seen to shake hands upon meeting.

Every animal that fights with its teeth lays back its ears when doing so.

LIFE EXPECTANCY

Most animals are said to have a life expectancy six times as long as their physical growth period. Or such be the claim of the science boys, at any rate. No doubt they mean barring ailments and accidents. Are most humans fully grown by age 18? Accordingly, if so, they should live to be 108.

Q. How many baby fish can a good mama guppy have at one time?

A. As many as 200. And some fancy fish folk say she can throw a litter, or whatever you call it, every two weeks.

ANIMAL ACT. Most dangerous animal act in the circus is not that of the lions and the tigers. It's the performance of the trained bears. Second most dangerous, any show put on by fully grown chimpanzees. Such is the contention of a trainer of lengthy experience.

A skunk never sprays into the wind.

ZOOS. If it's a well-kept zoo, the animals therein probably produce a sizable number of offspring. That's how the experts judge the quality of the zoo. By the breeding. Unhappy beasts don't reproduce.

It's a rare monkey that isn't exceedingly nearsighted.

LOOSE HORNS

Question arose as to why the horns on a rodeo bull appeared to hang loose and flap. That happens sometimes when a hornless breed of cattle is bred to horned cattle. Angus to Brahma, for instance. Calves therefrom sometimes have horns attached to the skin but not to the skull. Rodeo hands call them banana horns. Breeders call them scurs. False horns sometimes are strapped onto steers for roping, heading, heeling. But not onto bulls. Those bulls already have all the advantage they need. So reports a Texas expert.

Q. How big is a newly born black bear cub?

A. About the size of a grownup red squirrel. Weighs maybe eight ounces (227 g).

198

LIONS AND TIGERS

That the typical tiger is a fiercer fighter than the typical lion is common knowledge. Less widely known is what gives that tiger the advantage. Simple thing. The lion stands on three paws to maul with the fourth. But the tiger balances itself on its hind legs to maul with both front paws simultaneously. Moment by moment, the fighting paws on the tiger's side generally outnumber the fighting paws on the lion's side by two to one.

Q. In the wilds, do the lion and the tiger always fight when they meet?

A. Maybe they might. If they ever came face to face. Which they don't. They've sort of divided up the world's hunting grounds, never sharing same.

Bear in mind, you can always tell one lion from another by the pattern of whisker holes on their noses. Get right up there real close and take a look. Go ahead.

The unborn human baby starts to grow its first teeth within three months after conception.

That animal most often stuffed by a taxidermist is the bobcat.

Q. When somebody asked you if anybody ever milked an elk, you said it has been done. Where? When? By whom, pray?

A. What, you don't know? Why, Scythian women were milking elks as far back as 200 B.C.

The Siamese fighting fish would rather challenge its own reflection in a mirror than another Siamese fighting fish. That has been proved. Why is a mystery.

Average time lapse between the mosquito bite and the ensuing itch is three minutes. It's a fact. Biologists went to great lengths to find that out. What it means is almost no mosquito that requires more than three minutes to finish a meal survives.

Q. Is it conceivable a polar bear would ever mate with a brown bear?

A. Conceivable indeed. Bear cubs were born to such an unsegregated couple in the Washington zoo, as I recall.

Two out of five grizzly bear cubs die within 18 months of birth.

Do you realize that grownup male musk oxen eat only about a sixth as much as do cattle?

Q. Do skunks eat chickens?

A. Not usually. When the science boys examined the innards of 1,000 skunks from the wild, they found that less than 1 per cent contained poultry remains.

Those fighting tusk teeth of the hippopotamus continue to grow as long as the beast lives.

Q. Is there such a thing as a cross between a lion and a leopard?

A. Is indeed. In Tokyo's Hanshin Park Zoo live some leopons. As big as lions, but spotted like leopards. And elsewhere there are ligers, too. Half lions, half tigers. The foregoing facts destroy my erroneous notion earlier that the mule was the only species that could survive even though entirely killed off.

Argument continues as to whether any animal besides man either laughs or cries. A scientific fellow named Yerkes contends none other sheds tears in sorrow. But he insists apes do indeed laugh.

If that baby hippopotamus manages to survive its first year, it can be expected to live to about age 45. However, a lot of vicious beasts go after the hippo calves with the intent to do bodily harm. Crocodiles, for instance. And hippo bulls, too. Still, about four out of five do grow up.

It's said bees are most inclined to sting people on exceedingly windy days.

Q. What's the most dangerous wild animal in Africa?

A. Can only report the crocodile kills more people there than any other beast.

It's common knowledge a goat doesn't really like to eat tin cans, but chews the labels off them to get to the paste thereunder. Still, the belief a goat will devour just about everything is widespread. Now an animal trainer of some renown says otherwise. That goat really is a pretty finicky eater, he says. If you have the smell of something objectionable such as gasoline on your hands when you handle a goat's food, it flat out won't eat it.

Do lions, like housecats, enjoy catnip? Immensely!

ELEPHANTS

Elephants pull their own teeth. At least some do. By manipulating big sticks with their trunks. One such pachyderm named Peggy in a Pretoria, South Africa zoo thus extracted a three-pound molar. Did you know an elephant in its lifetime gets six to eight sets of molars?

Did I tell you an elephant keeper customarily cleans up that animal's hide with a blow torch?

BEAST BRIEFS. Average lion lives ten years . . . a baby kangaroo is only an inch long.

The younger the expectant father, the more likely the baby will be a boy.

MORE ELEPHANTS

Claim is that an elephant's hearing is so acute it can hear the tread of a mouse. Interesting, if true.

Q. Can a cobra kill an elephant?

A. If it bites the tip of the elephant's trunk or the base of the elephant's toenail, it can.

Q. Some rhinoceroses have two horns, right?

A. Indian rhinos do. African rhinos have one.

The telephone poles in many parts of Kenya and Uganda are higher than such poles hereabouts, a lot higher, to allow for giraffes.

WHICH WAY THE WIND BLOWS. Only the nose of a cow has sweat glands. That's why said cow faces into the wind on hot days. To keep cool. And faces away from the wind on cold days. To keep warm. Believe I told you all good pilots know this. They observe cattle to figure out which way the wind blows at ground level.

MEAN MINK. Am advised researchers at Michigan State are trying to cross the mean mink with the gentler ferret. To get the mink's rich coat without the bestial disposition. Seriously, they say they expect to call the new animal a merret, if the experiment succeeds, and a fink, if it doesn't.

Record shows that most of the man-eating lions in Africa—and it has been documented that there've been quite a many—tend to be slightly smaller than other lions.

Q. Does a barnyard rooster have to be taught to crow?

A. No, even if born deaf, said rooster can sound off.

DOGS

A dog's pawprint is as individual as a human fingerprint.

It's commonly believed that a guide dog habitually tells its blind master where to go. That's wrong. The master tells the dog where to go, always. To the left, to the right, forward, so on. Dog's job is to move with its owner for safety's sake, that's all.

Don't call the fire department to get that kitten out of the tree. Send the mother cat up there. She'll lead it down. So advises an expert on felines.

Alligators can close their ears just as camels can close their noses.

ALCOHOLIC ANIMALS

The maroela berries of southern Africa are not alcoholic, as such. But they tend to ferment in the stomach of an animal that eats them. An elephant, for instance. A perfectly sober elephant, without compulsions or neuroses, might find himself flat-out loaded. Never saw one such. Just read about it. In this condition, said elephant reportedly walks funny and sometimes winds up leaning against a tree.

Another African animal known to get drunk intentionally on fermented berries is the lion. And the baboon more notoriously than any. An inebriated baboon reportedly turns belligerent. But a lion in this unwholesome condition is said to become kittenish. Among my numerous money-making notions is a plan to film at some distant future date a television wildlife special featuring a drunken lion with a one-ton ball of yarn.

Q. Do eagles eat ducks?

A. With relish. No, without relish. But they eat them. Eagles eat anything. Told you they have bad breath, didn't I? Just awful. Some say eagles nest on distant mountaintops as a social courtesy.

23 The Naked Eye

This is hardly measurable, but it's a scientific fact the noise in the street tends to make it more difficult to see the colors in traffic lights. When there's a lot of booming and banging at the intersection, the green light appears brighter, the red light dimmer. That's to the naked eye of the average person.

Just about every proverb in our language has its counterpart in Spanish. "When in Rome, do as the Romans do," translates, "Wherever you be, do as you see." "Tell it to the Marines," translates, "Take that bone to another dog." "Silence is golden," translates, "Flies never enter a closed mouth." "If the shoe fits, wear it," translates, "If it itches, scratch it." "Sleep on it," translates, "Consult your pillow about it."

PUPIL

If you like what you see, the pupil in your eye gets bigger. If you don't like what you see, it gets smaller. If you're just not interested, its size doesn't change. Medical researchers contend they now have proved the foregoing beyond doubt. It's no new claim, however. Some old-time gamblers, who wear eye shades when they play, insist they've known about it for years.

In the south of France is a municipality called Port Nature. It's not just a beach, not just a small colony, but an entire town wherein the residents go naked. Correct, they shop for groceries that way, visit the movies that way, drink and dine in nightclubs that way. The place is near that larger city called Cap d'Agde.

Pound for pound, you can get more cabbage off an acre (½ hectare) of ground than any other vegetable, if all grows well.

PERFECT FACE. Young lady, the distance from the tip of your nose to the end of your chin should be exactly one-third the length of your face. And from your hairline to the inner tips of your eyebrows, likewise one-third. And from the inner tips of your eyebrows to the end of your nose, also one-third. That is, if you're the one girl in 100 said to possess the perfect countenance. Such is the claim of a sculptor who has made an extensive study of feminine features.

Q. Which is the older—the pyramids of Egypt or the Great Wall of China?

A. The pyramids.

The skin on your body least sensitive to pain is that on your heel.

MEMORY

If you have to memorize something, better go at it in short spurts. Scholars who research these matters say the rests between the study periods tend to anchor in your head whatever it is you're trying to remember.

Memory is inherited.

RECEDING CHIN

Common is the belief that a receding chin betrays a weak character. Recent studies contradict that notion, however.

They purport to show that a receding chin frequently signifies impatience, enthusiasm and mental quickness. Put a large nose above that receding chin with a receding forehead above the nose, it's said, and what you get is a citizen capable of making swift decisions. Interesting, if true.

The embezzler rarely takes sick leave.

FAST START. Takes the average healthy young man 1.76 seconds to move 10 feet from a standing start. Average professional baseball player does it in 1.02 seconds.

Each eye of a duck has three eyelids.

POTATO. Remember, the potato is not the root of the plant, but the stem.

LEGS. Since Joe Namath started modeling pantyhose, questions arise as to whether any men really do have beautiful legs. Certainly, certainly. Such was proved sometime back in Goulburn, New South Wales, Australia. A fellow named Frederick Newling entered a beautiful-legs contest against numerous girls. He won.

BATHTUB BUILT FOR TWO. Many an early wooden bathtub was fitted with a shelf across the middle to hold food and drink. Oval in shape, said tub was designed so two people could face each other over that shelf, and dine. The practice was practical. To get the maximum out of a minimum of hot water. But it fell out of favor when Queen Victoria moved the morality of the western world.

EYE-TO-EYE. If you want to comb, brush or otherwise gussy up your dog, put the animal up on a table. That's the counsel of a professional canine currier. Evidently there's something about the altitude that simmers down a pup. Oftentimes a squirmy pet that won't behave when you bend over it will hold steady on an eye-to-eye level.

AT&T TAKE NOTE. It has been claimed that the paint color on the inside of telephone booths tends to affect the length of the phone conversations. Talkers are said to spend more time on the line in brown, gray or black surroundings. They reportedly speed up their dialogues considerably within walls that are white, red or yellow.

Third most popular hobby now—after coin collecting and photography—is tropical fish.

POOLS

The Germans have come up with a way to keep the water in their outdoor swimming pools comfortable even in freezing weather. Not with heaters. They float thousands of little plastic balls on the surface. They're so small, they don't get in the way of the swimmers at all. But they completely cover the water, insulating it to hold in its heat throughout the season. Nifty.

Q. What foreign city is most visited by U.S. travelers?

A. Tijuana, Mexico. By far.

MELTING POT. Not everybody realizes that Italians in New York City outnumber the Italians in Rome, and the Irish in New York City outnumber the Irish in Dublin, and the Jews in New York City outnumber the Jews in Tel Aviv.

The claim that no twin ever became famous has been proved wrong. But the contention that no twin ever was recognized to be a genius remains unrefuted.

Q. What breed of dog has the best eyesight?

A. The greyhound.

OWLS. Question arises as to whether owls can see in the daytime as well as at night, and if so, why they're more active at night. Yes, they do see in the light, and exceedingly well, too. No big mystery why they hunt at night. That's when what they hunt comes out.

The new day does not begin exactly at midnight. Among the meteorologists, midnight is 00:00. They say the new day begins at 00:0001.

It used to be a good hotel, but that proves nothing—I used to be a good boy.

Mark Twain

Our Language man continues to add to his list of redundancies with "basic fundamentals," "coal black" and "soaking wet."

A great nose indicates a great man.

Edmond Rostand

Here's a report on those genes that determine the shapes of our noses. A happy report, too, if old Edmond Rostand got it right. Radical genes produce the decidedly different noses. Prominent noses, particularly. Conservative genes turn out the moderate straight noses. And it's a scientific fact the radical dominates the conservative. In other words, our noses from generation to generation tend to become more spectacular, not less so. Clearly, we're getting greater.

Maybe you didn't know that a scallop has about 35 eyes.

Q. There are three Tripolis in the Mediterranean area, in Libya, Lebanon and Greece. Phoenicians founded all three in 700 B.C. Which one do the marines refer to when they sing "From the Halls of Montezuma to the Shores of Tripoli?"

A. The one in Libya. Tripoli means "three cities," incidentally.

Nobody has ever seen a real ostrich stick its head in the sand, I'm told. A lot of people, though, have seen ostriches in the face of danger drop to the ground, stretch their necks far forward against the dirt, and watch intently.

In Heaven an angel is nobody in particular.

G. B. Shaw

ACOUSTICS

In Syracuse, Sicily, is an enormous bell-shaped cavern called the Ear of Dionysius. It's an acoustical marvel. About 400 B.C., the tyrant Dionysius made a dungeon out of that hole. And built his palace over it. Whatever his prisoners said, even in whispers, he could hear distinctly in one certain listening chamber above. Contention is that no other space on earth, not even the Mormon Tabernacle, is so fantastically fixed to focus sound.

Better keep your eyes open in the dentist's chair. Scientists recommend it, anyway. Because you're more aware of pain in the dark than in the daylight, they say.

That most common of cosmetic surgeries is the removal of extra tissue from baggy eyelids.

Q. How come chickens roost so early?

A. Because their night vision is bad. Very bad. Terrible.

CONTACT LENSES

Another innovation devised before its time by that genius Leonardo Da Vinci in 1508 was contact lenses.

Three out of four wearers of contact lenses are between 12 and 25 years old.

SHADES. Another little known fact is sunglasses were invented before writing. Ancient Africans made them out of bones. Early Alaskan natives used ivory.

TEETH

Were you aware that the enamel on your teeth is only about one-thousandth of an inch thick?

Did I tell you every human tooth has at least 50 miles (80 km) of canals in it?

INSECTS. No insect has ears on its head. Nor has any insect ever closed its eyes.

BY ANOTHER NAME . . . Firemen officially are now called firefighters. Newsboys are newspaper carriers. Craftsmen are craft workers. Clergymen are clergy. Public relations men are public relations specialists. And stewardesses are flight attendants. The U.S. Census Bureau says so. Got that?

Q. You said there's no record that Jesus ever laughed. Did he ever smile?

A. No record of that, either.

What can you tell about a person from looking at a photograph of same? Not much, evidently. Recent tests proved that neither intelligence nor personality traits show up with any consistency in plain photographs.

It's commonly claimed but rarely explained why elephants never forget. A little known fact about elephants is that they can't turn their heads to look behind them. They've just got to remember, possibly.

Was none other than that Assistant Secretary of Defense Henry Rowan who described the Pentagon as "a log going down the river with 25,000 ants on it, each thinking he's steering."

Do you have one of those electronic pocket calculators? If so, turn it on. And record side by side, not added up, each number mentioned in the following story. Exactly 7 Arab nations fought in a war. There were 107 men in each company. They battled for 73 days. In the end, only 45 men were left. Who won the war? Turn that calculator upside down to find out. Should read: "Shell Oil."

GROWTH. If you grew up from birth in a normal manner, your head doubled in size, your arms quadrupled in length, your legs quintupled in length, and your trunk tripled in length.

Q. How many hairs are in one eyebrow?

A. About 550, typically.

Q. How long does it take a plucked eyebrow hair to grow back?

A. About 92 days.

You don't send chrysanthemums in Italy. They're the symbol of death there.

212

Frequently reported is the contention that people with blue eyes are less sensitive to pain than are people with eyes of any other color. Client asks what eye color indicates the greatest sensitivity to pain. That's brown.

Medical specialists have verified the old contention that people with light gray, light blue or green eyes are more sensitive to glare than are people with brown eyes. They do indeed make better use of dark glasses.

Don't know if they do it anymore, but for many years it was traditional among the Chinese when talking to superiors to remove their eyeglasses, if any.

MELANIN. That pigment known as melanin is exactly the same both in blue eyes and black eyes. Doesn't look the same, does it? Difference comes from how the light reflects off the surface of the iris.

ADOPTIONS. Denmark has a central registry of all adoptions. It keeps track of the children, the adoptive parents and the natural parents, too. Scientific researchers from St. Louis went there to do a study of alcoholics. Question was whether children of alcoholics were themselves more likely to become alcoholics, even if adopted out so as to have no contact with the real parents. Answer was yes, incidence of alcoholism was twice as great among adopted children of alcoholics.

SEAGULLS. Did I tell you seagulls identify one another by the color of their eyes?

That ailment for which the most home remedies have been prescribed throughout history is said to be the sore throat.

BLACKBOARD JUNGLE. The color psychologists still insist that students in classrooms with yellow walls seem to make the better grades. Walls of pale gray or light blue are said to be good, too. But a classroom full of blackboards, they claim, is apt to make the students restless and a bit unruly.

WRINKLES

Heavy smoking tends to wrinkle your face. Such is the contention of a California doctor. Extensive photographic studies of smokers and nonsmokers in almost all age groups, he claims, show the faces of smokers to be much more lined. Why? Nicotine is known to constrict the capillaries. Constricted capillaries are known to cut down the blood supply to the tissues. A cut-down blood supply is known to lessen the elasticity of skin. That's the roundabout reasoning of the researchers.

Why tight shoes tend to make a person eat more food I don't know, but some psychological tests indicate such to be the case. So the testers advised dieters to go barefooted. Shrug.

How many conversations do you join into every day? Said Roy S. Dunton: "It has been estimated that from the first 'Good morning' to the last 'Good night' the average man engages in approximately 30 conversations a day."

Q. Ask some gourmet how I should hold my wine glass. By the stem or by the bowl?

A. Chilled white wine, by the stem. Room temperature red wine, by the bowl. Such be the contention of the second gourmet I asked. The first said, "Right in the middle so the bottle won't slip out of the paper bag."

24 Beginning to Show Promise

Said that great French painter Renoir shortly before he died at 78: "What a pity I should have to go now just when I was beginning to show promise!"

Among Thomas Jefferson's numerous reasons for renown was the fact that he was the first president to wear long trousers.

JAMES SMITHSON. That Englishman born in France, James Smithson, the fellow who founded the Smithsonian Institution, not only never visited the United States, but never even wrote a letter to anybody there.

Please note, Sir Isaac Newton ranks No. 468 on our list of the world's most bashful men. So shy was Sir Isaac that friends had to beg, bully and bamboozle him into publishing details of his most valuable discoveries.

Waterloo was the place Wellington used as a dateline for his dispatches. His victory over Napoleon actually occurred four miles (6.4 km) from there. Between the villages of Mont St. Jean and Pancenart. Napoleon didn't really meet his Waterloo at Waterloo.

CARRIE. If that temperance terror Carrie Nation wasn't primarily after publicity to promote her program, why was it that the first saloon she chose to chop up with her hatchet in 1901 belonged to heavyweight champion John L. Sullivan?

Count Volta sounds like a character in a horror movie, doesn't he? But no, he was the bright fellow who invented the electric battery. Make mention of this because a client asks the origin of the word volt. It was devised to honor the Count.

Q. Name the first child of European parents to be born in North America.

A. That was a lad called Snorro. In 1008 or thereabouts. His father was Thorfinn Karlsefni. His mother, Gudrid, was the widow of Leif Ericson's brother.

BIG EATER. That musical master named Handel was quite an eater. At a tavern, for instance, he liked to order dinner for three. Records show a waiter once told him that the grub would be ready as soon as his company showed up. And Handel reportedly said, "Good, so bring it right now. I'm the company."

Odd coincidence. John Adams and Thomas Jefferson, the only two U.S. presidents to sign the Declaration of Independence, died on the same day, namely on the 50th anniversary of that Declaration, July 4, 1826.

Q. How many U.S. presidents have been Unitarians?

A. Four. Both Adamses, Fillmore and Taft. Jefferson, too, was known to favor the Unitarian, but he said he didn't belong to any church.

ASSASSINATION. Before their assassinations, Abraham Lincoln's secretary, whose name was Kennedy, advised him not to go, and John F. Kennedy's secretary, whose name was Lincoln, advised him not to go.

MARITAL CHESS

King Ferrand of Portugal was held captive from 1213 to 1226 by the Turks. They demanded ransom. But Portugal's Queen Jeanne refused to pay for her husband's return. She had beaten him in a chess game, and he had therefore hit her on the nose with his fist. It upset her considerably. This is Item 81C in our Love and War man's file labeled "Hell Hath No Fury."

The great trial lawyer Clarence Darrow smoked cigars. In courtrooms, too, where allowed. He frequently lit up shortly before the prosecution started its argument. Invariably then, he sat motionless while the cigar ash grew longer and longer. A reporter, who observed this little trick repeatedly, finally realized that the attention of the jurors always seemed to shift from the prosecution talk to that lengthy cigar ash as they waited for it to drop. Notion even arose that Darrow ran a wire through his cigar to hold the ash in place. Who knows?

Q. The name of that old comic book hero "The Shadow" was Lamont Cranston, right?

A. That was the name his friend Cranston gave him permission to use. His own name was Kent Allard. Why the name change? Who knows? Da Shadow, he know.

A few generations ago, fly fronts replaced the sidebutton rectangular panels on gentlemen's trousers. But Mormon leader Brigham Young denounced the new pants design as an evil abomination. He forbid the men in his church to wear such.

Q. Who started the Kraft Cheese Company?

A. A fellow named Kraft, unsurprisingly. J. L. Kraft. In 1903. In Chicago. With $65 to rent a horse named Paddy. And a wagon. And enough left over to buy a small stock of cheese.

The elderly Henry Ford once examined some sugar crystals in a microscope. Throughout his life thereafter, he refused to eat granulated sugar, expressing the notion that it might cut up his innards.

Q. Quick, Louie, what did these famous men have in common? John Paul Jones, Ulysses S. Grant and Winston Churchill.

A. Each was exactly six inches (15 cm) taller than Napoleon Bonaparte who was 5-foot-1 (155 cm). What else they had in common was that thing called drive.

So what is Dr. Albert Einstein's epitaph? There's none. No marker, stone, plate, sign. Nothing with the remains. Such is what he ordered.

Q. Has any American president died of cancer?

A. Ulysses S. Grant did. Know of none other. Speaking of Grant, incidentally, it was at his presidential nomination that a fellow named Roscoe Conkling coined that still popular phrase: "Let the chips fall where they may."

Q. Who was the first U.S. president to have a phone on his desk?

A. Herbert Hoover.

TWO-PARTY SYSTEM. Students of politics ask whether the United States has ever had a president and vice president belonging to different political parties. Yes, when Federalist John Adams was president, his vice president was Republican Thomas Jefferson.

FAMOUS DOGS. Any Seasoned Citizen can tell you that Fala was the most famous dog of Franklin D. Roosevelt, but not one in a million recalls the name of F.D.R.'s other dog, Medworth.

The original plans for the Washington monument called for it to be five feet (152 cm) taller than it is now. And it was supposed to be ringed with an enormous Greek temple. The builders kept running out of funds. They finally gave up on the temple altogether. Took them 29 years to cap the thing.

Alexander Graham Bell invented the telephone in 1876, true enough. But credit Thomas A. Edison with the invention of long distance. Bell's device only carried three miles (5 km). Two years after Edison got his hands on it, it could send signals almost unlimited distances.

Q. Who first dreamed up daylight saving time?

A. Benjamin Franklin is credited with suggesting that citizens set the clocks ahead an hour to lengthen the days, but he regarded the suggestion as humorous.

Recall our Apt Epitaphs contest? Mrs. Fritzie Nauss of Wrightsville, Pennsylvania, suggests: "Ben Franklin, born, 1706 AC, died 1790 DC." And: "William Tell, Jr., Missed by His Father."

GEMINIS

The only Gemini ever to serve as a U.S. president was John F. Kennedy. Geminis are said to consider this unfortunate. They're thought to be a fairly sensitive bunch, and there are those among them who resent the fact that five Scorpios have become presidents. And four each of the Capricorns, Aquarians, Pisceans, and Taureans. They're aware, too, that the presidents have included three each of the Librans, Sagittarians and Cancers. And two each of Aries, Leo and Virgo. They console themselves only with the knowledge that a great many of the brainier presidential advisers have been Geminis.

What, you thought the real name of Billy the Kid was William H. Bonney? So did I. Wrong again! His real name was Henry McCarty.

THE SECRET OF LONG LIFE? It was at age 102 that the late George Motz of Kamiah, Idaho, said, "I got where I am by avoiding blondes."

Most common first moniker of U.S. presidents is James. Six were so named.

Here's to Samuel Slater—clink!—father of New England's textile industry. And he did his remarkable thing at the youthful age of 21. Slater was an apprentice in the Arkwright mills of Derbyshire, England. In 1789, he sneaked aboard a ship America bound, empty pocketed, under an assumed name. What a memory had that young man! With no specs, no blueprints—no nothing—he recreated in precise detail an entire cotton spinning mill at Pawtucket, Rhode Island. His project piloted others.

CAESAR

The word "caesar" originally meant "much hair." So it's odd, isn't it, that the most famous Caesar of them all, Julius, went bald?

First giraffe ever seen in Europe was sent to Rome from Egypt by none other than Julius Caesar.

SAN SALVADOR

It's commonly claimed that Christopher Columbus first set foot this side of the Atlantic on the island of San Salvador. In fact, a marble cross there commemorates the notion. Hardly any of the islanders believe it, however. They say no sailor in his right mind would have tried such a landing there.

And don't forget, Frederick the Great always insisted his coffee be made with champagne instead of water.

Q. How old were Caesar and Cleopatra when they were romancing?

A. He, 54. She, 21.

CLEOPATRA. It's the claim of a coin expert named Edward Rochette that the great Cleopatra was ugly. A piece of money was minted in Egypt during her reign there from 50 to 30 B.C. It shows her features to be almost grotesque. Rochette says those ancient coins were quite accurate. He also said it's highly doubtful a queen with Cleopatra's power would permit coinmakers to portray her as the possessor of forbidding features unless in fact she was downright homely.

CHOU EN-LAI. It's a matter of record that Dr. Henry Kissinger several years ago asked Chou En-lai to theorize on what might have happened if Nikita Khrushchev had been assassinated instead of John F. Kennedy. Chou reportedly mulled it a moment and said, "I don't believe Mr. Onassis would have married Mrs. Khrushchev."

THE EDISON PENCIL

A little-known fact about the great Thomas A. Edison is that he designed for himself a special pencil. The Eagle Pencil Company manufactured it to Edison's specs. Was about three inches long. With exceedingly soft black lead. In a wooden casing the size of a man's finger. Why Edison wanted exactly that particular scribble stick was he liked to carry it in his vest pocket. Previous pencils always stuck out, fell out or poked holes.

Just about everybody knows John Hancock was first to sign the Declaration of Independence. But how many know who the second signer was? Samuel Adams.

BEN FRANKLIN

It's almost universally known that old Ben Franklin used a kite and a key to experiment with the electricity in lightning. Less widely known is why he wasn't knocked cattywampus when that electrical charge zipped down the wet kite string. Ben didn't hold onto that string. He insulated himself from the end with a long silk ribbon. And stood under cover so the ribbon wouldn't get wet. In 1752 when a Russian scientist named Richman tried to repeat Franklin's experiment, he neglected to use that dry silk ribbon, and died.

As to what Benjamin Franklin's key opened—that key he used in his kite-lightning experiment—understand now it unlocked his cellar door.

SHORTHAND. John Robert Gregg was only 18 years old when he devised what some experts regard as the world's most nearly perfect shorthand alphabet. John was working in a law office at the time. Almost 100 years ago, it was.

It's claimed by some that Saint Luke recorded the Sermon on the Mount in shorthand.

CONFUCIUS. Everybody knows something about Confucius, but not everybody knows he was the eleventh child of a 70-year-old soldier.

CUSTER. James Warner Bellah's biography of General Custer in its entirety reads: "To put it mildly, this was an oddball."

25 World's Last Dodo Bird

When did the world's last dodo bird die? In 1681, that was. The same year that John Bunyan published "The Pilgrim's Progress." And William Penn took proprietorship over that acreage where the pretty deer play now known as Pennsylvania.

THE MARX BROTHERS

A customer asks about the infamous potato roast of the Marx brothers. That occurred in the office suite of MGM producer Irving Thalberg. The brothers, then four, got a little restless when Thalberg kept them waiting for 20 minutes in the outer room. So they sent out for a bag of spuds. And a half hour later, when Thalberg strolled out of his sanctum, he witnessed the four of them, sitting stark naked around his fireplace, roasting those potatoes. It is writ that Thalberg did not keep the Marx men waiting at any future date.

NO REFLEXES. What the animal experts are trying to figure out now is why that beast known as the sloth can't be startled by a loud noise. Just about every other animal can be scared into twitching, jerking, jumping. But no, not the sloth. Peculiar lack of reflex. Tap its knee with a rubber hammer and what do you get? Nothing.

That some humpback whales sing is common knowledge. Less widely known is the fact that they sing in accents which indicate where they're from. There's a Bahamas accent, a Puerto Rico accent, a Virgin Island accent. Or such be the contention of a University of Rhode Island oceanographer. Claim is those whales sing to one another from as far as 20 miles apart.

Put two hens in front of a pile of grain. Each will eat three times as much as either would eat if she were there alone. Scientific research has proved that.

Do you know how farm chickens get their vitamin D? From the sunshine through their combs.

Q. Will a queen bee sting you?

A. Not unless you're another queen bee.

Should somebody ask you to name the only mammal with a poisonous bite, say "the short-tailed shrew," and go on to other matters.

Many is the official city fire engine in Paris that's just a motorcycle under two men with an extinguisher.

Oh, and for those who prefer to buy in bulk, might mention that house flies weigh about 100,000 to the pound (454 g).

Are most professional salesmen born under the zodiac sign of Leo? Writes Mrs. Ina Stewart of Boise, Idaho: "During one year, I asked 132 salesmen who entered our shop to name their birth signs, and 122 said Leo. I'm convinced."

One out of every seven birds is some kind of finch. Finches live all over. Except in Australia. Aren't any there. I don't know why. Some birds in Australia are called finches, but that's wrong.

Q. Can eating too many carrots make your skin turn orange?

A. Can indeed. That carotene poisoning is called hypercarinosis. It won't kill you. And it will go away, if you lay off the carrots for a while.

So you're a pretty good talker, are you? All right, repeat this three times: "Sue's Snapshot Shop."

GROUNDS FOR DIVORCE

Numerous are the complaints in our Love and War man's file labeled "Grounds for Divorce." But he much prefers the more imaginative reports therein. Like the one about the Frenchwoman who was given her liberty after she told the judge that her husband played the bagpipes and made her keep time with a flyswatter.

OF TALL MEN

A particularly short fellow named James Howell in A.D. 1621 said: "Tall men are like houses of four stories, wherein commonly the uppermost room is worst furnished." Not long after that, another short character named Francis Bacon said: "Nature did never put her precious jewels into a garret four stories high, and therefore exceeding tall men had ever very empty heads." And just a little later, still one more man said: "Often the cockloft is empty in those whom Nature hath built many stories high." As a semi-tall sort of citizen, I resent these remarks, though not much.

OF TURKEYS

If you see a farmer carrying a long stick with a small red rag attached to one end of it, what kind of farmer would you expect him to be? Turkey farmer is the answer. Why turkeys respond so well to red is a mystery, but they do, and that flagged stick is what the farmers use to move those birds around under control.

That domesticated beast with the lowest Intelligence Quotient is said to be the turkey.

Do you know how farmers teach baby turkeys to eat? Put marbles into the feed. The little birds peck at the marbles. Their bills slide off into the mash. They get enough grub by accident to stay alive.

Birds that fly most everywhere are said to be considerably smarter than birds that walk a lot. Why I don't know. But take crows or woodpeckers. Alongside chickens and turkeys, they're practically brilliant.

When birds drink: A hummingbird laps with its tongue like a cat. A pigeon or dove sips like a kid with a soda straw. Just about any other bird fills its bill and tosses it back like a cowboy at the bar.

227

A ping-pong ball outweighs a hummingbird's nest, keep in mind.

FAITHFUL WOLF. Was customary when I was a lad to dub any flirtatious fellow as a wolf. How odd! It's now known that the wolf, of course, is an ideal mate. Marries for life. Doesn't chase. Further, he cleans up the den, hauls home his kills to feed the troops, and posts himself as guard over the whole shebang. He cares, the wolf does. Deeply.

DUCK. No matter how high the bridge, a goose, when walking under same, will lower its head. This is also true of every person who gets out of a helicopter, you'll note.

PACHYDERM VERSATILITY

It's told that a United Nations committee was formed to do a study on elephants. Representatives were appointed from France, West Germany, Great Britain, the Soviet Union, the United States and Denmark. Each submitted a paper, entitled as follows: France, "The Love of the Elephant." West Germany, "The Philosophy of the Elephant." Great Britain, "The Elephant, Its Contribution to the Growth of the Empire." The Soviet Union, "A Five-Year Plan for Elephants." The United States, "Bigger and Better Elephants." And Denmark, "How to Make 215 Different Kinds of Sandwiches Out of an Elephant."

Originally the leader of the Ku Klux Klan was not known as the Imperial Wizard but as the Grand Cyclops.

MOTHER GOOSE

Did I say the original Mother Goose was a Boston lady named Elizabeth Foster Goose born in 1665? "Wrong!" cries a scholarly client. "All evidence indicates that the Mother Goose legend originated in France long before that Boston woman was even born. There is a reference to Mother Goose in a French poem of 1650. And the Frenchman Perrault, that famous teller of fairy tales, referred to her, too."

228

Can't explain why the soul searchers continue to ask, "Which came first, the chicken or the egg?" The egg, naturally. Millions of same were laid by fishes, reptiles and other birds before chickens ever showed up, no?

LIMERICK

Highly pleased to report the limerick contest has drawn another offering. This, by Carlin Aden of Tacoma, Washington.

There was a young fellow named Flynn
Who had a large mouth but no chin.
He happened to slip
When he tried a back flip,
And darned if he didn't fall in.

BARNUM

Circus impresario P. T. Barnum for years kept beside his desk a large box labeled "Not to be opened until after the death of P. T. Barnum." Story was it contained a bequest for each of his employees. And the notion did something to hypodermic their daily labors, believe me. Day after Barnum died, they stood around with great expectations. The box was opened and everybody thereabouts was handed a copy of Barnum's autobiography. That was it, his last bit of bunk.

Q. How long does it take a chicken-plucking machine to remove all the feathers of the chicken?

A. About 14 seconds, I'm told.

Maybe you're not aware that some chicken breeders now are turning out featherless fowl. Utterly naked, those birds. They're said to be 16 per cent meatier than the same breed of chickens with feathers. It's unfortunate, though understandable, certainly, that they catch cold easily.

SMOKING

Cancer researchers at a Glasgow hospital in Scotland tried to teach mice to smoke cigarettes. The little beasts wouldn't cooperate. So the researchers switched to chickens. At first, the hens didn't cotton to it. But pretty soon they got hooked. Now there's a whole coop full of birds over there that evidence irritability if they don't each get half a cigarette every other day.

The marketing boys say each of us will have eaten 2,400 chickens, about, by the time we get to age 70.

HEADBANGERS

Far more baby boys than baby girls indulge in that intriguing pastime of banging their heads against walls. In fact, about three and a half times as many boys as girls do it, studies show. Usually, they start just under 8 months of age, and hang in there, banging away, until they're about 3½ years old. Indications are that only about seven per cent of all babies can be described as such head bangers. And they generally are said to be easy-going, trouble-free youngsters who hardly ever cry.

DON'T SCARE YOUR BIRD

Writes a lady subscriber: "You said my canary would start to sing if I put a mirror next to its cage. So I used my husband's shaving mirror, which magnifies greatly. Its enormous reflection terrified my little bird. It died. Please warn everybody."

It's a matter of record that numerous parakeets have been shocked to sudden death by the noise of firecrackers.

The American cuckoo doesn't cuckoo. Just clucks.

More than half the chickens in the U.S. come from fewer than 20 chicken growers.

Average hen lays 227 eggs a year.

Another common expression that doesn't hold up is that phrase "mad as a wet hen." Lot of poultry men on blazing hot days turn on cold showers in their coops. And the hens reportedly love that.

Certainly you know the bald eagle isn't.

The head keeper at the Frankfurt Zoo in West Germany rigged up a television set in front of the gorillas' cages. Just to see if it would influence the romantic activity of said beasts. It didn't. But careful observers who kept records found out something else. That the gorillas developed certain preferences in their viewing. In descending order, they seem to like love scenes, weight lifting and auto racing.

Q. What's that fish with hands?

A. The gurnard. It's also got feet and wings. Or so I'm told by an authority who has not always been wrong.

Do you know why you couldn't fly, even if you had wings? Your breastbone isn't strong enough.

SEASONED. You may call yourself a Seasoned Citizen if you recall when: 1. The biggest evening at the movies was "Bank Night." 2. When all the hearses were Packards. 3. An agricultural expert with the government during World War II suggested farmers remove the horses' shoes at night to save the metal.

BAKER ANTS. An ant called the Dalmatie chews grain into dough, shapes it into patties, then cooks same in the sun. So far as I know, this is the only beast, besides man, that bakes its own biscuits.

BLADDERWORT. Did you hear about the bladderwort? It's an underwater plant. It eats baby fish.

STATURE. Was none other than C. H. Brower who said, "A man of stature has no need of status." He is the fellow who also said, "You can't sink someone else's end of the boat and keep your own afloat." And "Chicken Little acted before her research was completed."

26 Now You Know

GIFT

This bride and groom got a particularly big batch of wedding presents. Among them was a pair of theater tickets with a note written in lipstick: "Guess who sent them?" Shrug. Didn't matter, they used said tickets that weekend, enjoyed the play immensely, and returned after midnight to find their apartment cleaned out completely, all the gifts gone. Scrawled on the bathroom mirror in lipstick was the flip message: "Now you know."

CLASSIFIED. Just came up with my new favorite classified ad. It reads: "Public announcements: Phi Beta Kappa will hold its next meeting Tuesday. Place: Conference Room, Central Library. Time: When the little hand is over the seven and the big hand is over the 12."

Black sheep have a sharper sense of smell than do white sheep.

EGGSHELL. If the shell on that egg is particularly hard to break, you can be fairly certain the hen that laid it was scared by something that day.

THE SADDEST TALE. Only one out of every 40 kites sold ever gets into the air.

Studies show a goldfish would rather look at a mirror than at another goldfish.

BANANAS. Bananas breathe. They inhale oxygen, exhale carbon dioxide, and generate their own heat.

As greetings, both handshaking and kissing are mighty popular hereabouts, that's obvious. It is a fact, however, that nose rubbing has been used more widely as a greeting than either handshaking or kissing throughout the history of mankind.

Don't know what else they do or how, but it is a matter of record that romantic Canadian porcupines kiss one another on the lips.

APHRODISIAC. That one natural food most widely claimed throughout history to be an aphrodisiac is honey.

ECONOMIC HEADACHES. When the economy is flourishing, people with pains go to doctors. But when a recession hits, they're more likely to treat themselves with aspirin, then wait. Thus, according to a medico who's made a lengthy study of the matter, the sale of aspirin is a fair economic barometer. Rising sales mean bad times. This is just the opposite to the significance of the sales of pencils. When they go up, good times are thought to be at hand.

MARKED CARDS. Simple matter to identify marked cards. Hold the deck in the left hand. Bend it sharply. Riffle the cards so you can see almost half of the backs of all the cards as they snap flat again. The back design on an unmarked deck will stand still. With a marked deck, shapes on those backs will shift and jump. Gambling expert John Scarne devised this minor detective trick.

Those slot machines that belong to the Las Vegas County Airport gross considerably more than the landing fees, don't you know. But that's nothing. When they were first installed by Western Airlines, it was rapidly revealed their take exceeded by somewhat even the revenue from passenger travel.

CAN'T ADD TWO AND TWO. If you draw a blank everytime you tackle a mathematical problem, what you suffer from is something called acalculia. Condolences.

No doubt you've seen countless cents-off coupons on countless products of countless manufacturers. But do you know who originated them? C. W. Post was the bright fellow. In 1895. He offered a one-cent discount coupon to introduce "Grape Nuts."

One half of knowing what you want is knowing what you have to give up to get it.

Sidney Howard

Client asks how it happened that the colony of Virginia came to be known as "The Mother of States." That's easily explained. Eventually, parts of it were turned into parts of Illinois, Indiana, Kentucky, Michigan, Minnesota, Ohio, West Virginia and Wisconsin.

Q. Was the great American tribal leader Sequoya a full-blooded Indian?

A. Not according to the record. His mother was part Cherokee. His father was an English trader named Nathaniel Gist. His mother brought him up. He never learned English. But he believed his English surname was Guess. Sequoya was the man, you'll recall, who devised a Cherokee alphabet, so is named as the creator of the first written language for the Indians.

Q. On the Cream of Wheat® packages is a picture of a smiling chef. Who was the model?

A. A Chicago waiter who worked at Kohlsaat's Restaurant

there. An early top executive of the Cream of Wheat Company, Emery Mapes noticed him one morning at breakfast. The waiter's genial smile and engaging manner clearly pleased his customers. Mapes offered him $5 to pose for the Cream of Wheat picture. By all means, said the waiter. And although his likeness has turned up on all Cream of Wheat boxes since then, his name remains unknown at the firm, as does his whereabouts.

Client asks our Love and War man why men tend to prefer blondes. Who said they do? Surveys repeatedly show that only about one man in every three prefers blondes.

Did you know that one out of every 10 dirty movies is filmed in Miami?

IVORY. Report is that the ivory tusks of 61,000 elephants were traded on world markets last year.

Do you know how Ivory Soap® came to be so called? In 1879, Harley Proctor, while at church, heard his minister drop the phrase "ivory palaces." Click! That simple.

Q. Who was the model for Uncle Sam in that famous "I Want You" poster of World War I?

A. The artist who designed the poster, James Montgomery Flagg.

So you think Mount Everest in the Himalayas is the highest mountain in the world, do you? So did I. But measured from the center of the earth, Mount Chimborazo in the Andes is higher. Credit the equatorial bulge for that.

Q. Who wears the longest beard in the world?

A. Nobody anymore. It's in the Smithsonian Institution. All 17½ feet (5⅓ meters) of it. A Norwegian named Hans Langseth grew it right up until he died in 1927.

To his list of redundancies, our Language man has added, "He shrugged his shoulders." Quite so.

CRIME PREVENTION. A retired police detective, who worked burglary for years, always hangs up his clothes on hangers hooked over the pole in alternative directions. Just habit, he says. It will prevent a thief, if any such turns up, from stripping his closet in one grab. But firemen advise against it, bear in mind.

A restaurateur of lengthy experience reports that women almost invariably take much longer than do men in the examination of a menu.

GIRLS AND PEARLS. Girls definitely are better pearl divers than men. That's been proved.

The product that sells best in U.S. supermarkets is toilet tissue. Exactly 98.2 per cent of the people use same, according to the trade publication *Progressive Grocer*. The magazine made no enlightening report about the other 1.8 per cent.

Three out of four firebugs are under age 21. And the boys among them outnumber the girls by 22 to one.

Q. What does the name "Hubert" mean?

A. Bright in spirit. The name explainers say men called Hubert are supposed to be happy, rollicking, jovial fellows. Watch this space for analyses of Henry, "home ruler"; George, "tiller of the soil"; Morris, "dark, Moorish," and Jimmy, "the supplanter." Expect, too, a rundown on Ronald, "mighty ruler" and Gerald, "mighty spearman."

TABU? In the ancient art of China are scenes depicting nakedness, brutality, even amorous acts in the extreme. But nowhere in said art is any painting of a woman's bare foot.

I've reported a lot of favorites here. Favorite limericks. Favorite classified ads. It would be an oversight to fail to report the favorite fortune cookie message which turned up in a Chinese restaurant in Syracuse, N.Y.: "You will meet a beautiful girl. You will give her money. She is our cashier."

Venetian blinds were not invented first by the Venetians, please note, but by the Japanese.

HIGH STEPPIN'

Men should wear high heels. To make their feet feel better. Or such be the claim of a university orthopedic surgeon. Men, too, might benefit some, if their weight were elevated from the balls of their feet upwards and backwards a smidgeon, according to this authority. That contention is not so hard to digest, if you've ever worn a good pair of cowboy boots. Those inch-and-a-half heels under soft leather skillfully stitched are remarkably gentle. I don't own any, yet. Intend to, though. Tried on a well-worn pair of a fitting friend recently and they seemed more comfortable than anything previously. Understand the technique of the stitching around the ankles is supposed to be highly significant. Why I don't know.

Approximately 1,000 beats per minute is typical of a canary's pulse.

About a third of your blood is in your legs at all times.

The older the patient, the longer said patient, during a stay in the doctor's office, visits with that professional. Whatever the age, though, about half of all patients spend less than 10 minutes in the actual presence of the esteemed being.

Remember, the lobster always enters its burrow tail first.

Various species of orchids grow on snow-covered mountain tops, too.

HOT DOG. In Frankfurt, beef-based sausages are called wieners in honor of that city known here as Vienna. In Vienna, beef-based sausages are called frankfurters in honor of that city known here as Frankfurt.

The slang word for a couldn't-care-less attitude in German is *Wurstigkeit* meaning "sausage-ism," but I don't know why.

239

AIR BATH. Historical footnotes say Benjamin Franklin habitually got up at daybreak to lounge around his bedchamber for a half hour or so stark naked. This he reportedly called his "air bath." It's said he believed it was just as refreshing as a water bath in the high-heeled-shoe tub he invented. Might try that.

Studies show that 70 per cent more men than women have to be rescued by lifeguards.

Q. Who invented cellophane?

A. One Jacques Edwin Bradenberger. In 1908. He was trying to make a tablecloth that wouldn't stain.

Q. Is Pearl Bailey tattooed?

A. She is. And so is Glen Campbell. But not in the same place. She wears a heart on her leg. He, a dagger on his arm.

Q. Who said, "Democracy is a form of religion, the worship of jackals by jackasses"? E. B. White?

A. No, H. L. Mencken. E. B. White said, "Democracy is the recurrent suspicion that more than half the people are right more than half the time."

27 Ups and Downs

If you like to ride on roller coasters, a philobat is what you are. If you can't stand them, you're an ocnophil.

It's a matter of record that some stunt pilots inexplicably suffer from motion sickness on such carnival rides as roller coasters.

Look at that beautiful palomino. Horses, I'm told, are the most hysterical of all domestic animals.

Q. Do submarines need more power to run at a given speed under water or on the surface?

A. On the surface. Now. But they used to use more power under water. Before the *Albacore* in 1953.

Ever been to Ireland's Blarney Castle? Understand the custodians there take excellent care of the famous Blarney Stone. Their first assignment every morning is to scrub yesterday's lipstick stains off the thing.

REMARRIAGE

Q. How many of those husbands and wives who get divorced remarry each other?

A. Figure about 10,000 a year in the U.S.A. alone.

Question also arises as to how frequently such remarriages of divorced couples work out in a happy manner. Research has been done on that, too. In a study of 200 such matrimonial mates, it was found half claimed happiness the second time around. But the rest were not too sure, not too sure at all.

It's another remarkable fact of nature that a squirrel can climb a tree faster than it can run on level ground.

What, you can't identify that condition called the postprandial dip? It's what prompts the Latins to take a siesta in the early afternoon. That after-lunch slump. Pretty common, isn't it? Yawn.

No, the guitar is not the most popular instrument among amateur musicians. Only 28 per cent of them pluck those strings. The piano is still at the top. About 46 per cent of the musical amateurs play it.

Q. Why are you always supposed to get up on a horse from its left side?

A. That ancient custom was started by mounted soldiers. Most were right-handed. So they wore their sword scabbards on the left. They had to swing up from the left to keep the scabbards from getting in the way.

Why do some whales commit suicide? Dr. James Glen Mead of the Smithsonian Institution reportedly discovered that pilot whales sometimes get parasitic roundworms in their inner ears. This knocks out their navigational savvy, so they blunder onto beaches to become stranded.

OPEN WIDE. It's conceivable that a youngster four feet (120 cm) tall could stand upright in the open mouth of a hippopotamus. Briefly.

As to its number of earthquakes, no doubt you know Japan ranks No. 1 in the world. But can you name the nation that rates No. 2? Neither could I. It's Italy, turns out.

" 'Now we're even,' said Steven, as he gave his wife five blows." Jonathan Swift wrote that. Report this in reply to a customer who wants to know where we got the term "Even Steven." That's where.

Average man stops growing when he's 21 years 2 months old. Average girl stops growing when she's 17 years 3 months old. Or so recent studies indicate.

That the flamingo sticks its whole head underwater to scoop for shrimp, snails, whatever, that's not the item. The item is its neck is so flexible that it turns some 180 degrees to stick its head into the water upside down.

First bird domesticated by man was not the chicken, but the goose, sir.

Q. What's a "rockoon?"

A. A combination rocket and balloon. Weathermen use such to boost measuring instruments 60 miles (96 km) high.

Were all the paved airport runways in Florida laid end to end, they'd make a highway 20 feet (6 meters) wide from Miami to Sitka, Alaska.

A student of the mind claims watchmakers, chefs and violinists tend to have the hottest tempers.

HANGOVER. Eat some activated charcoal. That will cure your hangover, if any. Or such is the claim of a medical fellow. Impurities in liquor, not the alcohol, are said to be what cause that awful ailment. And activated charcoal is thought to absorb said impurities. I don't know, Clyde . . .

Q. How many times does the average person fall in love before marriage?

A. Seven times, insist the experts. That sounds high.

Am asked how fast your blood passes through your heart. Depends. Get exercised and it can pour along at a rate of about four gallons a minute. That's as fast as water runs out of an ordinary kitchen faucet.

When you and I were tots we knew that canned vegetables cost a lot more than fresh vegetables. Not anymore. Canned vegetables cost about 70 per cent less these days. Blame spoilage in shipping.

WORST MONTHS

It's no news that January and February are the worst months for catching cold. But the winter weather isn't to blame, at least not directly. They're the worst months in Southern California and Florida, too. Some medical scholars credit the gathering together of the Christmas crowds as the chief cause for the spread of the viruses. March invariably shows a general letup of sniffles even though the weather often stays bitter then.

Q. How many feathers on a canary, friend?

A. About 2,200, average.

Average American in a lifetime moves approximately 14 times. Average Englander, about eight times. Average Japanese, maybe five times.

Another professional who tends to develop an immunity to seasickness is the train conductor.

Q. What do you call the constant fear of falling down stairs?

A. Cremnophobia. None too common, that one.

BACKACHE

If you are normal, presumably your back aches. Or at least it aches some of the time. The medical statisticians report that 80 per cent of the U.S. population experiences said low back pain. And they contend that anything experienced by 80 per cent of the population has to be considered normal.

If you work in any sort of office at all, chances are you'll spend at least 20 years of your life sitting down.

Best place to catch a butterfly is when said winged critter is sitting on a thistle. Insect specialists say butterflies actually get a little drunk on thistle nectar.

Q. I know there's catnip, but is there such a thing as dognip?

A. There is. A weed called Stinking Goose Foot. Smells terrible. But dogs tend to go into a high rapture when they hit a patch of it.

Imagine you've read about what upset the two fleas so greatly. The mortgage company turned down their loan application for a dog.

RELIGION

In an earlier day, one Professor George Washington Gale of Knox College stopped by a roadside inn to spend the night. Inquired the innkeeper: "Sir, I see you're a clergyman. Which be it? A Presbyterian or a Methodist?" The professor looked puzzled. Said the innkeeper: "I asked because it's my experience that a Presbyterian minister is exceedingly particular about his own food and bed while a Methodist is always concerned about the feed and care of his horse." "Of course," said the professor, "well, my man, I'm a Presbyterian, but my horse is a Methodist."

Nobody ever listened himself out of a job.

Calvin Coolidge

BED AND SHOES. If you ask a doctor to name the most important piece of furniture in your home, odds run 97 to one he'll say your bed. If you ask him to identify your most important attire, chances are about the same he'll say your shoes.

SAD SOUNDS

Laboratory scientists can produce high-pitched sounds which can cause the listener to feel hot and to ache all over. Also, they can turn out sounds which can make the listener inexplicably sad, even though said sounds are pitched too low for the human ear. What they're trying to figure out now is whether such bass noises occur unintentionally in cities, whether industry and traffic generate these, and whether great batches of people therefore become blue, melancholy, depressed, without realizing why.

HAVE A SEAT. Record shows that Alice Roosevelt Longworth once embroidered on a davenport pillow in her living room the following: "If you can't say something good about someone, sit right here by me."

SAFETY

An insurance statistician reports the summer season consistently is the most hazardous time of year.

Safest of the home playground equipment is the seesaw. Most dangerous is the swing set. Or so the researchers contend after a study of the 50,000 emergency room cases involving children.

Now, to his list of redundancies, our Language man has added "old adage" and "Rio Grande River."

HAIR. On any given day, one out of every 10 hairs on your head has stopped growing, it's said.

That place on your body where you're most likely to be stung by an insect is the foot.

Q. Those stagecoach stops in the Old West—how far apart were they?

A. Maybe 20 miles (32 km).

Numerous restaurants in Argentina customarily serve a pair of dice with each meal, I'm told. Loser pays.

Three high school boys skipped the first two classes, then told the teacher they were late because the one car they brought had a flat. "All right," she said, "but you'll need to take a make-up test for the work you missed this morning." She seated them apart. And in its entirety, her make-up test, written out on the blackboard, read: "Which tire went flat?" Tricky. Very tricky.

Q. Did Nero really play the fiddle while Rome burned?

A. What historians think he played was an instrument called the lyre fidicula. They say he was about 35 miles away from the fire when it broke out. He hot-footed it into Rome immediately to boss the firefighters and help those burned out. Then he set up his headquarters in the Trans-Tiber area which remained clear of the blaze. And one night observers reportedly saw him on the roof of his pavilion, watching the flames on the skyline. They say he picked up his fidicula and sang a variation of the blues about it all. I gather the word fidicula led to our word fiddle.

INTERNAL CLOCK. Do you know at what time of day or night you were born? Theory is spreading that your birth sets your physical clocks to ticking, thus determining at the outset whether you were to be a day or night person. If you were born around dawn, you're thought to do your best work in the early morning. But if you were born in the late afternoon, you're not expected to perk up really until the evening. Or so goes the notion.

28 Is Your Celery Wilted?

CELERY. Is your celery wilted? All right, slice a spud into cold water, add the celery, and let stand for an hour. That ought to crisp it up.

SALAD

Q. Why does that lady on TV say never cut lettuce, always tear it?

A. Am told the cut edges tend to "rust," but the torn edges don't.

CAESAR SALAD

You're familiar with Caesar salad, but can you identify the Caesar for whom said dish was named? Caesar Cardini, inn-keeper of Tijuana, Mexico, it was. Over 50 years ago on July 4, Señor Cardini's eatery ran out of grub. Big crowd that weekend. All he could find in the ice chest were a couple of crates of romaine lettuce, a half crate of eggs, some four-day-old pullman bread, lemons, romano cheese and spices. He invented.

Q. Where is Caesar Cardini now?

A. In Los Angeles, last I heard. Manufacturing a dressing for said salad. Incidentally, an informant reports it was not

Caesar but his older brother Alexander who actually created that famous salad. Who knows?

You say you don't know how to get all the meat out of the coconut shell? Nothing to it. Pierce the eyes with an ice pick. Drain the milk. Bake the coconut for 25 minutes in a 350-degree F. (230°-C.) oven. Then put the coconut in the freezer for an hour. Just a couple of taps with a hammer now will crack the shell, leaving the meat intact.

You can wind up with an onion-flavored omelet just by storing the unbroken eggs in the onion bin, realize that?

EGGS

Q. How can you tell whether an egg is fresh without breaking the shell?

A. Put it in a pan of cool salty water. If it sinks, it's infant new. If it hovers, it's middle-aged. If it rises, it's old before its time.

The fresher the hard-boiled egg, the more difficult it is to peel. You know that. But do you know why? A newly laid egg with a white that's more acidic than alkaline has an adhesive quality. But an egg that's a few days old becomes more alkaline than acidic, and loses that stickiness. Scientists learned that about 20 years ago, probably after your mother found it out.

Another good way to get egg stains off silverware is to rub them with damp salt.

Say you store a bushel of potatoes in a plastic bag. If you put just one apple in there, too, it will give off enough ethylene gas to stop the bud growth on all those spuds.

A dash of salt over your dish of ice cream will bring out the flavor, you know.

To his list of redundancies, our Language man has added "rehash."

Q. How do you make tiger's milk?

A. Nothing to it. Take a quart of milk, two teaspoonfuls of brewer's yeast, a half cup of soy flour and a half can of frozen orange juice. Mix it all up in a blender. That's it.

Remember, in the freezer, garlic flavors get stronger, chili flavors get weaker.

Q. How do you clear up iced tea that's real cloudy?

A. Splash in a couple of shots of boiling water.

You won't cry when you peel onions, if you whistle continuously. So reports a lady client who says she has proved it repeatedly.

A difficult zipper, if not stuck completely, will slide more easily if you rub it with a soft lead pencil.

If you don't like the odor of cooking brussels sprouts, toss a piece of bread in the pot, suggests one chef.

Q. When broiling, should I leave the oven open or closed?

A. With electricity, slightly ajar. With gas, closed. Seems the gas burns up the smoke and tends to dry things out, but the electricity does otherwise. Or so the experts report.

Take apple butter. Under the heretofore secret regulations of the U.S. Food and Drug Administration, any four ounces of same marketed to the public ought not contain more than five dead insects. Popcorn is not supposed to harbor more than two rat hairs per pound. And as for coffee beans, the rule is nine out of 10 shouldn't be moldy. Good news, what?

Q. How many pounds of potato chips can I get out of 100 pounds (45 kg) of potatoes?

A. About 25 pounds (11 kg). Counting the 12 pounds of oil they're fried in.

BREAKING IN NEW SHOES. Here's a way the lumberjack gets a perfect fit in his new boots. Before ever working in them, he fills them with water to soak overnight. Next morning, he puts them on wet, wears them all day, letting them dry to the form of his feet. Then he softens up the leather with a little bear grease. And their excellent new shape never changes thereafter.

Roses cut in the afternoon last considerably longer than roses cut in the morning.

PERENNIALS. If you dip the stems of cut flowers into hot water before you put them into cold water, they'll last a lot longer.

Q. How do you make one of those beautiful pineapple plants?

A. Slice off the crown. Place it, cut side down, in a saucer of water. Later, after it grows a little, find some sunny place to replant it in sandy soil.

HOUSE PLANTS. She bakes the potting soil before she puts her house plants in it, this lady. For about half an hour in a 180-degree (82° Celsius) oven. Kills fungi, she claims.

If your thermometer is hard to shake down, it's defective, remember that.

BATS. Only mammal besides man that carries its lunch with it on a day-long trip is the bat. Curls its tail into a pouch full of insects so it can feed in flight.

Roasted, one average size man would serve about 60 cannibals, though not heartily. Anthropologists at the University of Michigan figured that out. All right, I believe that's enough.

If you intend to make a spice cake for freezing, better leave out the cloves. In cold storage, that clove gets stronger and stronger and stronger.

Put that hot cake pan on a damp cloth for a few seconds if you want the cake to come out easily.

WICKER. Lot of people don't realize that wicker lawn furniture lasts longer if it's rained on periodically.

You can keep tools from rusting by putting mothballs in your tool chest.

Carry a can of cream of tartar in your car. Sprinkle a little on the windshield. Smear it around. Let it set a minute, then wipe clean. It will keep the wipers from smearing for up to 200 miles (320 km).

Not much works better to snazzy up the family brass than a paste of lemon juice and cream of tartar.

LEMONS

Q. Which half of the lemon should I save when I only want to use half a lemon?
A. Save the stem half. It'll last longer.

Roll the lemon under your palm on a hard surface. Poke a hole in it with a toothpick. Then squeeze out just a few drops of juice to tasty up a mixed drink. That's how the beautiful people do it now.

254

Am thinking of writing a "How To" book for souls who want to get rid of ants. Be a pretty short book, though. Just sprinkle cucumber peelings around. Zip, the ants will go away, goodbye, so long, get lost.

ROACHES. Am repeatedly asked what's the best way to get rid of roaches. Simple. Sprinkle boric acid powder round-about. Powerful poisons scare those roaches off, temporarily, before they're contaminated. Boric acid powder is subtler. Takes it a couple of weeks to get to the little beasts. And they don't realize they're being done in.

Next to a bottle of warm formula, nothing so satisfactorily simmers down a fussy baby as a feather dipped in molasses. Place the feather in the infant's fist. Done? The fascinated child, who heretofore devoted most of the time trying to grab ahold of things, now devotes all the time trying to let go. And oh so silently. This tale was told to me by an old wife.

Hot coffee is what's most apt to burn a child accidentally. The statisticians found that out in a 17-year study. Most dangerous day is Tuesday. They say they don't know why. Most dangerous time of day is the dinner hour.

If your toddler's white shoelaces won't stay tied, starch them.

NEVER, NEVER. Never start a long hike in new boots. Never buy a perfectly waterproof sleeping bag. Never build an outdoor cookfire bigger than the frying pan. Those are only three "nevers" for the backpackers. Can you come up with any others?

Mix a hefty dash of ordinary meat tenderizer with a table-spoonful of water. Rub that on your chigger welts, mosquito bites and bee stings. Away goes the pain! That's because the tenderizer contains an enzyme called papain. It promptly neutralizes such venoms.

HINTS. The Household Hints experts advise: 1. Shine your bathroom chrome with rubbing alcohol. 2. Bury old banana peels around your rose bushes. And 3. Count on a dozen ice cubes per guest at your next party.

If you want your ice cubes to come out crystal clear, pour hot, not cold water into the trays.

CORKER. Among the 83 known ways to get a stuck cork out of a bottle is that technique which calls for you to wrap a cloth dipped into boiling water around the bottle neck to expand the gases therein and thus force said cork loose.

You know how hot dishes sometimes leave marks on table tops? Am advised not much works better to remove said marks than a rubdown with a thin paste of salt and salad oil.

COFFEE STAINS. Yes, it's true that coffee stains on wooden floors will come clean, if rubbed gently with steel wool and alcohol.

Not many people realize that Tabasco sauce is a superb silver polish.

What, you can't get that tar off your hands? Rub the spots with grapefruit, orange or lemon peel.

Do you have any liquid starch around the house, young lady? Put a few tablespoons of it in the warm soapsuds you use to scrub the linoleum floor. Really makes it shine.

TEA. If you steep old tea leaves in water for half an hour, then strain the liquid, that tea works excellently well to clean varnished woodwork, mirrors, window panes.

Q. Has anybody ever figured out how much dirt is wiped, swept and vacuumed out of the average home every week?

256

A. That, too, has been calculated. About nine ounces.

PIANO TUNING. Query arises as to exactly what a piano tuner listens for when he works on a piano. First, he taps a steel tuning fork against his knee. Vibrating 440 times a second, it produces the tone he wants to hear from the piano's middle A string, which he tightens or loosens to get a tone match with the fork. The rest of the piano keys he tunes from that middle A pitch.

STAINS

If you can't get the stained sink white again with a little scouring powder and chlorine bleach, try this. Make a paste with cream of tartar and hydrogen peroxide and scrub that on the stain with a hand brush.

If you are having trouble keeping your handkerchiefs bright white, soak them for a half hour in a pan of cold water wherein you've dissolved a teaspoonful of cream of tartar. That's said to work in a dandy manner.

If you paint an old hemline mark with white vinegar, it will iron out easily.

That gallon of white paint will cover a lot better if you toss a couple of ounces of lamp black into it.

What, you hate to clean the oil-based paint out of a brush when you have to stop in the middle of a job? Why bother? Just put that brush in a plastic wrapper and freeze it. When you want to start painting again, thaw it out for 30 minutes, then have at it.

It is a good thing that life is not as serious as it seems to a waiter.

Don Herold

A scholar named Dexter examined the school records in Denver. Specifically, the frequency with which youngsters were punished for acting up. Then he compared said records with the weather charts. Lo, he found, when the humidity was over 80, the children were chewed out five times as often as when the humidity was below 45. Significant, what?

JUDGE NOT A BOOK BY ITS COVER. It has been reported that food packaged in green sells best. Toys packaged in green, however, sell least well. Or so the toymakers report. They say red is their best package color, with blue second.

Nine out of every 10 people reported missing turn up of their own accord.

BABY FAT? If that chubby youngster doesn't slim down by age 7, it's likely said citizen will stay fat for a lifetime. So reports that English medical journal called *Practitioner*.

Q. How come coffee pots are always tall and thin while teapots are always short and fat?

A. Work better that way. Coffee grounds sink in hot water. Tea leaves rise to expand.

All the members in one tribe of Malaya, the Bajaus, are born on small boats where they live out their lives, rocking on the water. On those rare occasions when some selected few go ashore, they almost invariably get earthsick. Dizzy. Nauseous. Or so a man of science reports.

Nothing complicated about a little sewing needle, is there? Still, it goes through the hands of about 20 craftsmen who give it more than that many manufacturing processes.

Q. I know a hen's egg should be stored small end down, but why?

A. Because the air pocket inside it is in the large end. Were it stored downward, it would tend to rise upward, unstabilizing the egg.

THE NOSE KNOWS. Most sensitive part of your body to pressure is not your fingertips, as widely believed, but your nose. You don't think so? Touch your fingertip to your nose. You'll see which registers the pressure first.

SOMETHING OLD, SOMETHING NEW

Some things are better after the new wears off, after they're broken in, after they've endured a season: Leather boots, a desk chair, rose bushes, asphalt paving, or a typewriter. And some things are never better than when they're just unwrapped, diminished not a whit, unmarked by fingerprints and dust, whistling crisp: A ream of white paper, a bar of soap, a box of bullets, a cord of firewood, or a barnful of baled hay.

Q. Who said, "Trust everybody, but cut the cards"? Cromwell?

A. No, Finley Peter Dunne said that. Cromwell said, "Trust in God and keep your powder dry."

What makes popcorn pop? Pressure inside the hard shell? No, sir, cut a kernel in half and both halves will pop. Baffling.

Next time you get all shook up—by shook up I mean happy, blue, angry, whatever—put your fingertips to your cheek. It's likely they'll feel a bit chilled.

It was none other than Dr. Karl Menninger who explained the difference between neurotic and psychotic as follows: "Neurotic means he's not as sensible as I am. Psychotic means he's even worse than my brother-in-law."

29 Nobody's Perfect

In the battle for existence, talent is the punch and tact is the clever footwork.

Wilson Mizner

If you want to distinguish the penguin from all other birds in the world, simply say it's the only one that can swim but not fly.

Warm-water fishes make a lot more noises than cold-water fishes, bear in mind.

Told you that Moses was a stutterer, but did I mention that Aristotle was, too?

DAWN OF A NEW DAY

One out of every 10 people eats breakfast out.

One out of every five grownups skips breakfast.

Among birds, only the owl can detect the color blue, experts say.

Chinese experts say even a good math student needs about five years to become proficient at handling that oriental device known as the abacus.

COMPLAINTS, COMPLAINTS. Most common complaint by patients to their doctors is, "I'm having trouble breathing," or words to that effect, describing respiratory infections. Second most common complaint is, "I've got a pain in my back."

Q. How many times did the old Pony Express riders fail to get the mail through?

A. Only once. And they covered that 2,000-mile (3,200-km) route for 19 months. Pretty fair record.

There's a billboard in Massachusetts which reads: "Road closed—do not enter!" The other side reads: "Welcome back, stupid!"

What do you mean, "pure as the driven snow"? Driven snow is never pure. Only the snow made in laboratories is.

UNDER THE SEA

Feed a penguin fresh water, and more often than not, said bird will get sick.

Just about nothing natural is noisier underwater than a bed of shrimp.

Q. Will music attract honeybees?

A. Don't see how. Honeybees are deaf.

Can you breathe and swallow at the same time? Neither can I. But we could, once. Babies under half a year old do it all the time, then lose the knack.

Astereognosis, that's the name of one peculiar human abnormality. It's rare. The patient afflicted with same can't recognize the shape of anything just by touch alone. For instance, a pencil feels no different from a pineapple.

PAINT. Nobody has ever made a paint that's perfectly black or perfectly white.

It's claimed that people can work efficiently within a spread of only 35 Fahrenheit degrees (20 Celsius degrees) of temperature. That's from about 50 degrees F. (10°C.) to approximately 85 (30°C.) degrees F. Below 50, the muscles tend to stiffen up. Above 85, the thinking process gets sluggish. At this writing, it's evidently above 85.

The only venomous snake that will attack a human without provocation is the African Mamba.

The tiger, the gila monster, the wasp, each bears the distinctive colors of orange and black. And each is dangerous. To a greater or lesser degree. In the world of beasts, orange and black should be a signal for caution, say the wildlife scholars. Even the butterfly so marked, they say, tastes terrible.

Your hand is said to be normal if your thumb is as strong as the four fingers opposing it.

SUPER HEARING. Hyperacusia is an odd ailment of the ear. Sufferers of same develop a most acute sense of hearing. Some common little noises sound like cannon shots. Medicos report one victim of this disorder was able to hear the ticking of a wristwatch from 30 feet (9 meters) away.

MESSY HOUSE

What, you say you feel a little guilty because your house is a mess? Think nothing of it. A scholar who studies personality traits suggests that sloppy housekeeping is the sign of a creative mind. Dr. Donald Mackinnon is the authority here. He contends creative people try to find "a higher quality of orderliness," so can't be bothered with the insignificant scatter of unwashed socks, dirty ashtrays and dishes in the sink. Good news, no?

With palm stretched flat, if the tip of your little finger ends exactly at the last joint in your ring finger, you're normal. Check that.

HAIR SPLITTING. "Why," asked I, "do most men part their hair on the left?" "Because," replied a bright client, "most mothers are right-handed."

Let's see you try to describe a spiral staircase without using your hands. Go on. Try.

If you rub crushed garlic between your palms with sufficient vigor, you'll wind up with the odor of garlic on your breath.

The record shows one baby in New York City was named "Encore" because his father said "he wasn't scheduled on the program."

Q. What's the technical term for the sound of a growling stomach?

A. I don't want to talk about it. Oh, all right: "Borborygmi."

Maybe you didn't realize that a rat can go without water longer than a camel.

A groundhog never drinks water.

HICCOUGH FISH. There's a certain fish in South America's waters that gulps air and then belches so loudly it can be heard for miles. How gross! It's called the hiccough fish.

MEDICINE CHEST

What are the five most common items in a family medicine chest? A druggist says: Aspirin, adhesive bandages, a thermometer, an antibacterial ointment and some sort of topical antiseptic such as Mercurochrome, iodine or Merthiolate. Calls to mind the oft-repeated claim years ago of a Spokane city detective. He said he could find out more about a man by looking into his medicine chest than by reading his diary. I happened to notice in mine the other morning a yo-yo, an avocado seed and a snapshot of Alan Alda. What do you suppose he'd make of that?

The rodeo boys tell me that a good bucking horse only works about 10 minutes a year.

Both worker ants and honeybees just mope around doing nothing about half the time.

NAIL BITERS. Claim is that people with blue eyes and red hair are more likely to be nail biters than people with brown eyes and brown hair.

In Assyrian the word "adam" means "man."

Rabbits don't perspire. Neither do guinea pigs.

Q. Do pigs perspire?

A. No, people perspire. Pigs sweat. But only on their snouts. This testy reply comes from our Language man, that sensitive fellow.

That animal which tends to sweat the soonest and the most with the least amount of effort in proportion to its size is the horse.

There's no known instance wherein a crow ever flew in a straight line.

Only mammal that can't jump is said to be the elephant.

The typical cow devotes about 18 hours out of every 24 to chewing on something.

No true bug chews its food.

BEWARE OF DOG. That dangerous big cat known as the jaguar is said to be scared of all dogs no matter the size of same.

Maybe you already knew there are three times as many muscles in the tail of a cat as in the human hand and wrist.

A hog's eyesight is better than a human's.

Add to his other credits the fact that Benjamin Franklin was the fellow who first shipped rhubarb into the U.S.A.

COLD FEET. Not all historians realize that Thomas Jefferson soaked his feet every day in a tub of ice water.

Abe Lincoln always moved his lips when he read.

Not a bird in the world has fewer neckbones than the giraffe. Even the little English sparrow has 14. Credit the duck with 16. And the swan, 23. As you no doubt have read, the giraffe has only seven neckbones.

It is a rare man whose ears match.

Cabbages get hernias.

Q. Are any people ever born without fingerprints?

A. Has happened. Medical records indicate members through four generations of one Philadelphia family turned up without fingerprints. But there's no other such case known.

What, you had a bad day this week? Forget it. You know what Somerset Maugham said: "Only the mediocre man is always at his best."

30 You Can Housebreak an Armadillo

You can housebreak an armadillo, you know. This comes up because a client asks. And asks, also, how frequently a pet armadillo should be fed. Once a day at 9 p.m. Dog food will do. But the little rascal probably will like milk, eggs, berries, nuts and raw meat better.

An armadillo can walk underwater.

Q. Do rattlesnakes eat frogs?

A. No, rattlers make their grub out of warm-blooded animals only.

You cannot immediately see the footprints of a fly under a microscope. But you can see them a few hours later. As the bacteria in them grow. A fly swatter salesman told me that.

FIRE! Am asked how a horse, a cow and a mule are apt to behave in a burning barn. The horse will freeze, so needs to be blindfolded to be led out. The cow will walk out quietly enough with a couple of swats on the tail. But the mule without encouragement most likely will kick the door down to get away.

WATCH YOUR BIRD. Look, don't put that caged bird of yours near an open window. Experts contend that nothing, not even bad grub, is more likely to hurt such a fowl than a draft.

Why do cats purr? A feline expert contends it's what's left of an ancient mechanism to soothe kittens.

GORILLA

When a man folds his arms across his chest, it's generally understood to be a defensive gesture. He may do it in an argument, for instance, to show he intends to stand his ground. But when a gorilla folds his arms across his chest, that's something else. It's a gesture of submission, say the animal experts. Means the gorilla is giving up, won't fight back, intends no harm.

What's so remarkable about the pigeon is it's the only bird that can drink water without raising its head to swallow.

You can't tell whether your baby is too hot or too cold by touching its hands. They tend to be cold more often than not. That's because the blood is busy in the mid-section where the food is. Cold hands do not necessarily mean cold baby, not at all. Or so says a medical specialist. To find out if a baby is dressed too warmly or too lightly, he says, take a temperature with your fingertips between the shoulder blades.

SWEAT IT OFF. Have you been under the impression that you can lose weight by perspiring profusely? Likewise. But that's wrong, evidently. Or so says an authority with the U.S. Food and Drug Administration. It's thought to be the commonest misconception among dieters.

A color consultant of some renown contends the best hue for the walls of cafeterias is peach. Experience shows customers surrounded by peach order more servings and leave less food on their plates, this authority avers. White is said to be among the worst colors for cafeteria walls.

Are you aware that you're entitled to a full refund if the telegram you send is not delivered within five hours?

READER REPORT: "The fish's head was five inches (12.5 cm) long. Its tail was as long as its head and half its body. Its body was as long as its head and tail together. So how long was the fish?" That's what I asked. Exactly 40 inches (100 cm), report numerous callers.

How do you account for the fact that numerous people who lose all their teeth soon thereafter become at least partially deaf?

The gorilla has one more pair of ribs than a man.

Marriage is the alliance of two people, one of whom never remembers birthdays and the other who never forgets them.
Ogden Nash

That marine snail called the tethys is about a foot long. And when it lays eggs, sir, it lays eggs. About 40,000 a minute, in fact. In four months, it can lay 400 million. Do you realize that's almost two tethys's eggs for every man, woman and child in the U.S.A?

FISH

Fish make funny noises under water. You've heard that. Now here comes a fisherman of lengthy experience who contends those fish actually grunt, squeak, chatter to one another. So he lets the first one he catches swim around under his boat on a short leader. Swears that caught fish calls out to the others, bringing them in close.

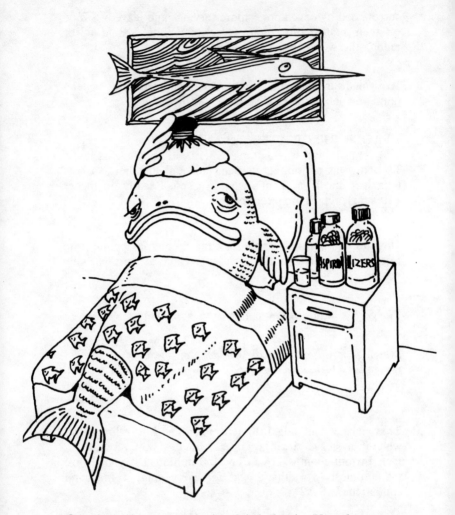

Question arises as to whether fish feel pain. Yes, the experts now say, fish certainly react physically to whatever hurts them. Their survival, like that of all animal life, depends on their capacity to feel pain. Whether they feel mental anguish as a result of pain, however, remains a mystery.

Most polar bears never set foot on land.

DOG AND CAT

Note it stated in print that a dog never feels ashamed of itself. Can't believe it. I've seen a poodle, clipped too short, go hide under a bed until his hair grew out. And a certain dalmatian frequently skulked away in obvious embarrassment when it skidded off course in a squirrel chase. It's true, however, that a cat never feels ashamed of itself.

Q. How deep should the water in a birdbath be?

A. Two and a half inches (63 mm). If deeper, it scares the birds. If shallower, it clumsies up their wash.

The blue satin bower bird of New Guinea mixes charcoal and berry juice, and with a piece of bark for a brush, paints the inside of its nest blue.

Sellers of goldfish nationwide annually peddle one such for every 3.5 citizens.

No angler who goes for catfish should overlook this remedy for the sting of the catfish barb. Rub the stung spot against the catfish's underside. The pain will let up right away.

Q. How do the sheep in Montana compare to the population there?

A. The sheep are dumber. Wait, that's too flip. About two sheep to each person.

Zoo animals need vacations, too. Lions, seals, pandas, that sort, they get sick and tired of all those people staring at them. Eventually, with no relief from the daily performance, they slink into hideaways and sulk. That's why the keepers of the Tokyo Zoo shut down the place for two months every year. They say the beasts need the break.

271

To his growing list of redundancies, our Language man now has added "tuna fish" and "grocery store."

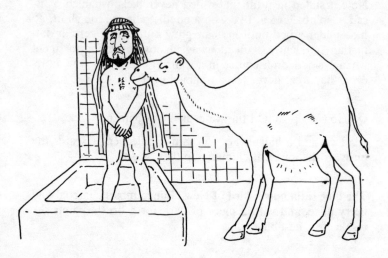

Q. Could a thirsty camel drink a whole bathtub full of water in one shot?

A. Easily.

OYSTERS

There's nothing in Christianity or Buddhism that quite matches the sympathetic unselfishness of an oyster.

H. H. Munro

World's first oyster farmer was said to be that old Roman gentleman named Sergius Orata, an entrepreneur of more than 2,000 years ago who seeded his own undersea beds. Whatever had to do with water was his specialty, I gather. He also invented the first shower bath.

Among those who fight to survive poisonous snakebites, up-dated statistics now indicate only three out of 100 don't make it.

BABOONS

If you walk toward a pack of baboons with a real gun over your shoulder, they'll scatter frantically. But if you walk toward them with a stick that looks like a gun, they won't be bluffed. How the beasts know the difference is what the animal experts are still trying to figure out. Those animal experts care more than I do.

ANIMAL MISCONCEPTIONS

No bear in a fight ever bearhugs. It slaps out. Flying fish aren't playing. They're fleeing from bigger fish. And cats do not particularly like cream. They only lap at it when there's nothing better to eat.

NO SWEET TOOTH. Have you ever seen a cat eat sugar? It's unlikely, contends a feline fancier, because cats can't perceive the taste of sweets.

You can grow a sword with the use of hormones on a swordless female swordfish, if you like.

If you get yourself a shrimp that's more than one year old, you've got an elderly shrimp, senator. One year is an exceedingly ripe old age for a shrimp. In fact, a year is the shrimp's traditional life cycle.

Our Love and War man is proud of the fact that Roget's Thesaurus lists 404 synonyms for "love" but only 107 synonyms for "hate."

A deer changes its bedding-down spot at least four times a night.

Q. How does a shark keep its teeth so sharp?

A. It sheds them. And grows them new. Continually. From

the rear of the mouth to the front. No row of old teeth lasts long enough to be worn down. And the new teeth are razor edged. South Pacific natives have been known to shave with them.

If put into a corral with a rhinoceros, which would you prefer as a weapon, a .45 caliber pistol or a baseball bat? A big game hunter of some experience says the bat might be best. When you hit a rhino solidly on the tip of its horn, you can knock it cold for about six seconds, he says. He thinks your chances of missing the horn tip are a little greater with a handgun.

MOTHER RAT. If a mother rat washes her newborn baby, she'll care for it thereafter, lovingly. If you wash it, she'll eat it, promptly. Now let's say no more about it.

Q. How many children as a general rule go on wetting the bed after age 4?

A. One in five. Those generally stop by the time they're 11. That's why a lot of quack bed-wetting cures make money. They get credit for the eventual success even though they might not have anything to do with it.

GREASE THE PALM. In the Robin Hood years, men rarely took baths, if ever. But they did perfume their palms with spiced goosegrease. It was expensive. So it became an acceptable gift, usually offered to some higher noble by a gentleman about to ask for a favor. Our Language man says that's the origin of the expression "to grease the palm."

How many pets do you have on your property? England's Queen Victoria had 83 dogs. She knew them all by name.

Since you were age 15, have you ever had a fist fight or a hair-pulling match? Pollsters put that query to numerous men and women. One out of every two men said yes. But only one out of every nine women said yes. Both the fist-fighting men and the hair-pulling women exhibited signs of mild pride when they replied, the pollsters said.

SIAMESE CATS

Was reported that Siamese cats for centuries in their native Thailand were trained to take the place of watchdogs. Client asks how such a little beast could possibly scare off any grownup human trespasser. Story is those cats were taught to sneak silently up behind an intruder, then jump on said intruder's back, digging in the claws just below the shoulder blades, thus to stay positioned so as to be a little hard to swat. That's the story.

Snakes, too, are known to be fairly particular about what they eat. That's to say one sort such as the green snake will eat crickets and grasshoppers, but won't touch lizards or mice. And another sort such as the water snake may eat fish and frogs, but won't have anything to do with insects or rodents. They specialize, those snakes.

COWS

When a dairyman budgets to build a new barn, he has to take into account the probability that his herd's milk production will fall off sharply when those cows get pushed into unfamiliar surroundings. It's also true that they tend to give less milk when a stranger milks them. That's why a dairyman who can't keep his hired hands on a permanent basis is liable to get into trouble.

Am acquainted with a farmer's wife who for years tossed all her dirty clothes into an old milk can about twice a week, added some soap and hot water, and let her husband heave the container onto the back of his pickup truck. His daily rounds took him over some pretty rough roads, she said. By sundown, the clothes were clean.

He who calls his pup to him for the purpose of punishing the little rascal teaches that dog never to come when it's called. That's bad. Very bad. So says a trainer of canines. You reward your dog by bringing it to you, contends this authority, and you punish it by sending it away.

Do you know where the candymakers get that licorice flavor they put into chewing gum? From an oil that's squeezed out of one of the 39 types of goldenrod.

Americans sell pork livers to the French who make expensive pate out of them and sell them back to the Americans. That's Item No. 81C in our file labeled "Pigs in World Trade."

Q. What are "zoonoses"?

A. Diseases that humans can catch from animals.

276

DOGS

Dogs brought up in England aren't as mean as dogs raised elsewhere. Go on, ask me how I found that out. Through a United Nations survey. It shows fewer British mailmen are bitten by dogs than postmen in any other nation, that's how.

That grasshoppers are edible is widely known. Less widely known is the fact that they are three times as nutritious pound for pound as beefsteak.

Spokesmen for the footwear factories say they couldn't get anybody to buy their fancy plastic shoes until they impregnated same with a synthetic odor of leather.

ELEPHANTS UNDERSTAND

Upon command, a good domesticated Asian elephant by age 25 ought to understand 24 separate orders. That's not counting the special kicks in the ribs from the rider. Said elephant also ought to be able to pick up from the ground on order these five things: a machete, an axe, a hobble chain, a coil of rope and a stick. This is an Asian elephant, remember. An African elephant is rarely trained for chores.

Her problem in Africa—I refer to the "Born Free" lady named Mrs. Joy Adamson—was hippopotamuses. They trampled her lawn. So she just rimmed the grass with a little low line of rocks, that's all. Hippopotamuses shuffle. They're averse to stepping over whatever.

Geese have been trained to tend sheep.

FENCE. The board of a certain Canadian school commissioned an old boy called Swede to build a fence around the place. Dandy fence, too, turned out. With a wide gate. But down in one corner, Swede cut a fair-sized hole in the thing. Board members asked why. "I know kids," said Swede. "Put a gate in, they'll climb over. This way, they'll go through the hole. Fence lasts longer."

31 The Red Baron

RED BARON

Anybody who has kept up with Snoopy in "Peanuts" knows about Rittmeister Manfred Freiherr von Richthofen, the famous Red Baron. But few realize that this German pilot of World War I was such a slow learner at the outset of his career that he cracked up not one but two airplanes during landings.

BRICKS. Each French aviator during World War I was required to carry a bag of bricks on every combat flight. To throw some of same, if the opportunity arose, into the propellers of German airplanes. The record shows two German airplanes were knocked out of the air in this manner.

It's the claim of one historian that the enormous majority of bullets fired in pistol duels missed their marks completely.

The deadliest form of dueling ever devised by man was a bit of bestiality called the Scandinavian belt duel. Opponents were stripped naked, fastened together with a strong belt so they faced each other about a foot apart, then handed short daggers.

BALDNESS

Recently quoted a renowned authority who claimed baldness is a sign of intelligence. But a client says that report was incomplete. In fact, it has long been believed that a man who gets bald across the front of his head is a thinker while a man who gets bald on the crown of his head is a lover. It follows, certainly, that a man who gets bald all over his head thinks he's a lover.

Mongolians rarely get bald. Likewise, American Indians. That's another big reason the anthropologists are certain the American Indians originally came from Mongolia.

If Alopecia were your ailment, you'd be bald, sir.

INDIANS

Q. Which of the Indian tribes killed the most whites?

A. The Kiowa, probably. With the Comanches.

Those military men who claim to know contend the best bow and arrow experts of all time were the Apache Indians. A good Apache bowman, they say, could keep eight arrows in the air, so quick was he to the quiver. And 100 yards (90 meters) was a typical range.

PANIC

Over 25 years ago, there was a terrible explosion in Perth Amboy, New Jersey, which stirred considerable panic. Wasn't until a milkman with a visor on his cap stepped forth to issue directions that the nervous crowd seemed to calm down. Scholars who looked into that disaster decided nothing so arouses confidence in an emergency as the appearance on the scene of somebody in a uniform. It is the contention of some of these experts that all schoolteachers should be so attired.

Q. Where'd we get the word "tycoon"?

A. From the Orient. Japanese: *taikun* meaning shogun. Chinese: *t'ai kiuan* meaning emperor.

Those turbans worn by Hindu sikhs are said to be better head protectors for motorcyclists than plastic helmets.

Q. In the lingo of the firemen, what's a "roast"?

A. A fire that takes lives.

BALANCE OF TRADE

Every now and then, some country buys so much of something from another country that the trade balance gets upset. Even as the United States now buys oil from the Middle East. This kind of dangerous imbalance has been cropping up for a long time. One of the most intriguing instances of it occurred during the 17th century when all the notables in France wore wigs. They imported bales and bales of horse hair for them from Germany. Colbert, the finance minister to Louis XIV, went into a snit for fear the Germans would get all the French gold. He tried to outlaw the wig, but couldn't pull it off.

TRAVEL TIPS. Travel experts in Tokyo have put out a booklet of tips to Japanese air tourists. Among other recommendations, it suggests passengers do not change into their pajamas in the airplane aisles. Maybe you recall hearing about that booklet. It's the one that also advises those passengers to face outward, not toward the wall, when seated in an American bathroom.

Takes less energy to fuel an airplane tank from the bottom than from the top.

FLYING HIGH

If you're going to take your infant on an airplane trip, make sure you feed said baby a bottle during takeoff and the landing. To equalize the pressure on the eardrums, don't you know.

If you want to find a good dentist, ask an airline pilot. A flyer has to be particularly cautious about the care of the teeth. If air is left in pockets under fillings, it expands at high altitudes. Understand that can be excruciatingly painful.

Q. Why is it more difficult for a dentist to extract lower teeth than uppers?

A. Because the lower jawbone is the most calcified, the hardest bone in the body.

BEES

No doubt you know the warriors of old used catapults to throw great rocks over the walls of the castles they attacked. Rocks were not their most effective weapon, however. It was when they catapulted beehives over those castle walls that they really stung the enemy inside.

282

In 1705, Britain was at war with France. One morning on the beach of West Hartlepool, England, citizens thereabouts watched an odd looking character climb out of a rowboat. The stranger was pretty hairy. It jabbered unintelligibly. Actually, it was an ape, previously the mascot of a wrecked ship. But those villagers weren't all that too familiar with apes. They court-martialed the beast, found it guilty, and hanged it as a French spy.

BACK IN THE AIR

Do you fly your own plane? If so, do you fly at least 300 hours a year? That's the break-even point, say the money-men. If you put in fewer air hours, they contend, you're better off to rent a plane whenever.

What, you thought the landing was harder on an airplane's wheels than the takeoff? So did I. But that's not right. The plane with its fuel load is heavier at the takeoff. Also, takeoff speed is a lot faster than landing speed.

Q. Tell me quick without looking—how old was Apache Chief Geronimo when the Indian fighters finally killed him?

A. Couldn't. Had to look it up. He was 80. But he wasn't a chief and nobody killed him. He died in 1909 on a farm at Fort Sill, Oklahoma.

What living thing most approaches an airplane in the manner in which it glides through the air? Scholars credit the flying fish with that distinction. Its flight fins remain fairly rigid.

ROYAL AIR FORCE

It's really a fact that the clothing of British pilots during World War II was outfitted with secret gadgets. To help said pilots, if shot down, escape from German prisons. Front of a trouser button, for instance, could be unscrewed to expose a miniature compass. Inside one shoelace was a sawtooth wire to cut through steel bars. One playing card in an official deck peeled open to reveal a scale map of Europe. No, these weren't nonsense notions dreamed up by the fiction boys. They were government issue. Quite real. Designed by one Major Clayton Hutton. And the record shows they helped about 3,000 British prisoners get free.

Q. Where do we get the term "bigwig" to describe a VIP?

A. King Louis XIV started that one. Why I don't know, but he decided it would be nifty to wear an enormous wig. Nobles throughout France did likewise, predictably. The nobler the noble, the bigger the wig. Wearers of little wigs or no wigs at all looked on admiringly.

It's against the law in India to fly an airplane over the Taj Mahal.

Crashes of airplanes piloted by women are exceedingly rare. Not just because there are fewer women pilots. Studies of flight mileages show the girls' safety record is about three times better than the men's.

Each suit in a deck of cards originally designated an occupational class. Hearts, the churchmen, Spades, the soldiers. Diamonds, the merchants, Clubs, the farmers. You'd think the soldiers would have been the clubs and the farmers the spades, what? Wasn't the case, however.

Q. Weren't there a lot of soldiers in the American Civil War who were just barely into their teens?

A. Not all that many. Of the 2,778,000 soldiers, only 252 were known to be under 15.

HE SHOULD HAVE BEEN A DOCTOR. Understand Napoleon's handwriting was something else. So bad, in fact, some of his letters were stolen by spies, not for what they said, but because they were thought to be maps of battlefields.

Q. When we hear something we can't believe, why do we say, "Tell it to the marines"?

A. Somebody told King Charles II of England about flying fish. He didn't believe there were such. However, his colonel of marines said flying fish did indeed exist. So the King decreed: "Doubtful reports henceforth shall be told to the marines, and if they verify them, we can safely consider them true." So says our Language man.

Q. Has anybody in the U.S.A. ever been both an Army general and a Navy admiral?

A. Only one man insofar as the record shows. Samuel Powhatan Carter. He put together the Tennessee Brigade, fought in the Civil War, rose to major general. By 1865, he started serving as a lieutenant commander on the gunboat *Mercury* on Asia station. In 1866, he retired from the Army. Later he went on up to rear admiral in the Navy before retiring again, in 1882.

Everybody's aware it was Julius Caesar who said, "I came. I saw. I conquered." But hardly anybody knows just where he came to, what he saw, and what he conquered: It was to Asia where he beat Pharnaces in the Battle of Zela. File that.

Jet lag affects you less when you fly west than when you fly east, and less than either when you fly north or south.

You've stayed in a hotel. No doubt a motel, too. Maybe even a boatel. But have you ever stayed in a "lotel"? Imagine so. It's what the Dutch call a hotel with a helicopter pad on the roof.

It was none other than the great Groucho Marx who suggested skyjackings can be stopped by giving each passenger upon boarding the airplane two parachutes and $500,000 in small unmarked bills.

LOONS. Every now and then in damp dark weather, that big bird known as the loon mistakenly lands on wet pavement, thinking it's a lake. Too bad. It's stuck. The loon can't take off from hard ground. Needs a water runway.

Most racecar drivers when off the track pilot big heavy cars and trucks rather than compacts.

Q. Why were German submarines called "U boats"?

A. For *Unterseeboot* meaning "underseaboat."

In Freiburg, Germany, stands a statue of a duck. During World War II, said duck quacked when Allied planes approached. Freiburg had other air raid signals, too, but none so reliable, it's said.

32 Faster than a Speeding Bullet

Am asked to name the most peculiar legislation I ever read. Hard to say. Still, that 1912 Nebraska law to control automotive traffic was a dilly. Required each driver on country roads at night to send up a skyrocket every 150 yards (135 meters), wait eight minutes for the road to clear, then drive on cautiously, blowing the horn while shooting off Roman candles.

A Detroit authority says nobody knows why the drivers of red automobiles are more likely to get into wrecks than are the drivers of any other color cars. But the accident statistics indicate such to be the case.

Were you aware there's a fellow in San Francisco who carries a homing pigeon in his car? Turns it loose when freeway traffic ties him up. So his wife will know he'll be late for dinner. Or so I'm told by a reader there.

A big computer can execute its operations so quickly that it would take one of same only about 20 minutes to calculate some bit of data about every person on earth.

Q. When I cough, how fast do I blow that little bit of air?

A. Depends. At its start deep in the windpipe, it moves almost as fast as sound. By the time it gets to your Adam's apple, it's down to hurricane velocity. And it's slowed up to about as fast as a horse can run when it flies by your teeth, if any.

METEORITES

Three meteorites, weighing at least 20 pounds (9 kg) each, fall to earth daily. That's the guess of the science boys. Further, they think one meteorite, weighing at least 4,000 tons (3,600 tonnes), falls to earth once every 100 years. And they believe one meteorite, weighing at least 40,000 tons (36,000 tonnes), falls to earth once every 1,000 years.

Meteorites are never round or flat.

Did you hear that a hog can run about 11 m.p.h. (17.6 km.p.h.)?

PIGS. Three months plus three weeks plus three days. That's how long it takes a female pig to become a mama. No other barnyard animal multiplies that quickly.

Q. If you were to figure the speed of Christopher Columbus' first transatlantic trip in miles per hour, how fast did he sail?

A. Say 2.8 m.p.h. (4.48 km.p.h.).

No sir, you cannot legally shave off your whiskers while driving a car in Massachusetts.

Those probers into privacy now report the average American working man makes six trips a day to the washroom.

Still hard to grasp the fact that more than eight million lightning strokes hit the earth somewhere on an average day.

288

Q. Can a giraffe outrun a horse?

A. Almost but not quite. In short sprints. A giraffe can't hold up long. Its lungs can only take in about 13 quarts (12.5 liters) of air in one breath. The horse's lungs can handle 33 quarts (31.5 liters).

That bird known as the roadrunner can move over the ground just about as fast as a race horse and maybe a little faster.

It's said that a certain land crab in Cuba can run faster than a horse.

Q. What time of day does your hair grow the fastest?

A. In the morning.

Q. How fast do whales swim?

A. About three to five m.p.h. (4.8 to 8 km.p.h.), most of them. Blue whales, though, can turn it on right up to 25 m.p.h. (40 km.p.h.), faster than any man can run.

Penguins can swim faster than the fastest men can run.

Q. How much faster is a cheetah than a man in the 100-yard (90-meter) dash?

A. Top cheetah speed, maybe 4.5 seconds. Top man speed, 9.1 seconds or thereabouts.

GLASS. If that piece of glass was formed by a lightning strike, it's called a fulgurite. If by a volcanic eruption, it's called obsidian. This comes up because a client asks where man first got the notion to make glass. From one of the foregoing, nobody knows which.

If the axis of the earth were a rocket tube from the South Pole to the North Pole, every second of every day and night it would be aimed to fire directly at the North Star.

CRAWLERS

The centipede, which is supposed to have 100 legs, only has about 40. The millipede, which is supposed to have 1,000 legs, only has 100, maybe 200. A centipede at top speed can carry itself on as few as four legs at a time. That millipede, though, keeps more legs on the ground than in the air. The centipede can move a lot faster than can a millipede in traveling, say, across the back of your neck.

The average flight speed of a housefly is approximately the same as that of a walking horse. Just 4.5 m.p.h. (7.2 km.p.h.) to be specific.

Takes a fifth of a second to blink your eye. And if you do it the way most people do it, you'll do it 20 times every minute. An ophthalmologist told me that.

Q. Why are some of the tollways called turnpikes?

A. Because the earliest of same were blocked off by long pike poles on pivots which were turned aside to let the travelers pass after the tolls were paid.

The law in Gainesville, Florida, decrees that no railroad train may roll through town faster than a man can walk.

It's a crime punishable by death in Alabama to put salt on a railroad track.

Q. How many parts in a car?

A. About 13,000 would be typical.

Q. What's "Amtrak" stand for?

A. "AMerican TRavel by trAcK."

In Japan now, the slang word for "motorcyclists" literally translated says "thunderbreed."

Am asked the most dangerous of the United States, statistically, to drive a car. California merits that distinction. Texas comes in second. New York, third. As reckoned by fatal smashups.

UNSAFE AUTOS. Half the cars that sail by you on the road in the U.S.A. are faulty in some way. How do I know? Because states which require auto inspections report that half fail to pass the first time. Worrisome notion.

Q. How long have the police been writing speeding tickets to car drivers in the U.S.?

A. About 71 years. The record shows the first motorist so ticketed was pulled over in 1904 at Newport, Rhode Island, for zipping along at 20 m.p.h. (32 km.p.h.), which was 5 m.p.h. over the limit. That driver was jailed for five days, it should be noted.

HOG

Vocabulary of the typical hog is about 20 words. No, not words exactly. But tones of oink. Studies at the University of Sussex indicate that. At any rate, the hog is far more conversational than, say, the cow or the horse. Pritnear loquacious, in fact.

Los Angeles Police sometime back set up an experimental race in four unmarked cars. Over a 10-mile stretch of the eight-lane Hollywood freeway. Three of the cars were permitted to go as fast as possible without changing lanes. The fourth was permitted to weave at will, switching lanes, jockeying for position. That fourth car made the trip in 15 minutes 30 seconds. The other three finished in another four seconds, 76 seconds and 82 seconds. That quickly. Illuminating.

Were you aware an ostrich can cover 25 feet (7.5 meters) in one stride?

Q. What sort of injury is most common among people hit by lightning?

A. A partial and temporary loss of hearing. Believe you already know that more lightning victims survive than die, no?

Q. How frequently does one bolt of lightning hit more than one person?

A. In three out of 10 strikes that hit somebody, more than one somebody gets hit each strike.

Q. Can an ostrich run as fast as a man?

A. Twice as fast. In spurts.

IN SPURTS

The spurt speed of a leatherback turtle in water is faster than any man can run.

University of Maryland researchers have determined that the spurt speed of a snail is three inches (7.6 centimeters) per minute.

33 The Last Word

Death of Senator Everett Dirksen left a vacuum none too easy to fill. After a campaign speech once, a lad ran up to him to say, "Senator, I wouldn't vote for you if you were Saint Peter!" Dirksen, pausing appropriately, replied, "Son, if I were Saint Peter, you wouldn't be in my district."

Astronomers claim there are more stars in the universe than grains of sand on the shores of this earth.

The scientists figure a hundred billion people have lived on this planet so far. They also figure there are about a hundred billion stars in our own galaxy. Curious coincidence. But pill or no pill, these figures are subject to change.

Little late in reporting this, but in the year 1816, most all the ponds in Vermont froze over on the Fourth of July.

Q. Where is that earthquake seam known as "McHenry's Fault"?

A. On the campus of the University of California at Santa Cruz. Named in honor of Chancellor Dean McHenry. Geology students there discovered it along with two others. They're named: "My Fault" and "Your Fault."

WHAT'S IN A NAME? Understand some professional men, originally known as "undertakers," now say they likewise don't much care to be known as "funeral directors," so prefer to call themselves "grief therapists."

When two dogs approach each other, you can tell before they meet which one is going to be in charge. It will be the pup that very slowly wags its tail as it walks up. Not that quick wag-wag-wag. Only the slow wag is known as the boss-dog sign. If both wag slowly, look out.

It's because of the drag of the tides against the earth's rotation that the days now are three hours longer than they were 400 million years ago. Another billion years, the days will be 30 hours long. Stand by.

In Africa, what's the most dangerous of all the animals, when wounded? The big-game boys say it's the leopard. It's not unusual, they say, for a wounded leopard first to vanish, then to turn and stalk, finally to attack the man who shot it.

Q. Are rats either right-handed or left-handed?

A. They are. And mostly right-handed.

That Saturday is the day of the week when the most fatal car crackups occur is generally known. That Wednesday is when the fewest happen, likewise. Year in and year out, approximately the same number of death wrecks are reported on Tuesday and Thursday. More than on Wednesday. But not so many as on Friday and Saturday. Wednesday is that day of the week when the fewest people drink.

READ ALL ABOUT IT

This shows how the news reports shape history. On Oct. 8, 1871, Chicago caught fire. And about 300 people died there. That same night, the logging town of Peshtigo, Wisconsin, likewise caught fire. As did the great forest around it. And about 1,150 died there. But Peshtigo's telegraph lines burned down. So the news was late getting out. And what with all the print about Chicago, there was little room left in the papers for stories on Peshtigo. Not one citizen in 1,000 is aware now that the Chicago fire was the lesser of that day's holocausts.

You know that little lizard called the chameleon? How do you suppose it stores its tongue? A chameleon only seven inches long has been seen to stick out its tongue 12 inches farther than its body length.

TELEPHONE MANNERS. Remember, if you're the one who dialed the telephone, good manners says you should be the one who ends the conversation. That's in social situations. Doesn't apply to crisp dialogues between you and your boss. Or so report the etiquette experts.

Item No. 68C in our Love and War man's file labeled "Happiness is" is a Chinese proverb which reads: "If you want to be happy for a few hours, get drunk. If you want to be happy for a weekend, get married. If you want to be happy for a week, butcher a pig. If you want to be happy all your life long, become a gardener."

Q. What's Fiddler's Green?

A. That's the sailors' Heaven. Incidentally, can you name any other occupational group that has its own private Hereafter? Neither can I.

Takes 72 different muscles to speak one word.

Q. Where'd we get the expression "kick the bucket"?

A. From ancient hangings. History texts say some early Americans, sentenced to be hanged, were made to stand atop buckets as the nooses around their necks were drawn taut. Thus to kick the bucket meant to die.

Am asked the world's most difficult language. Debatable. But the linguists frequently nominate Eskuara, the tongue spoken by the Basques in the Pyrenees Mountains. If you're not born into it, you'll never learn it. That's the Basque claim.

Thomas Jefferson wrote his own epitaph. In it, he identified himself as the founder of religious freedom in Virginia, the founder of the University of Virginia and the author of the Declaration of Independence. He made no mention therein of his two terms as president of the United States. Odd.

In Cripple Creek, Colorado, this epitaph appears on a natural rock tombstone: "He called Bill Smith a liar."

A client claims he saw the following epitaph on a tombstone in a Kentucky cemetery: "See. I told you I was sick."

LAST WILL AND TESTAMENT

It's a matter of record that a certain wealthy husband, whose wife threw a conniption every time he tried to smoke a cigar in the house, bequeathed to her $1 million in his last will and testament, on the condition she smoke five cigars a day. Another final statement, probated in Scotland, left nothing more to one widow than a handkerchief into which she was supposed to cry. And a third such death document by a London barrister offered his bereaved matrimonial mate not only all the accounts receivable from his firm, but the personal services in the entire of that firm's chief clerk.

It was in Kentucky where a woman sued a neighbor lady for $75 minus $45. The $75, she said, was for damages she suffered as the target of abusive language. The $45, she allowed, was a credit for what she yelled back.

Q. A friendly neighbor asked me to do a minor repair job as a favor, and I said, sure, I'll be over on the next fifth Saturday in February, if not too busy. So when will that be?

A. Mark your calendar for Feb. 29, 1992, sir. If you can't make it then, reset the appointment for Feb. 29, 2020.

Almost half the practicing psychiatrists admit they've been attacked at one time or another by patients.

There are so many preservatives in the foods we eat of late that our bodies do not deteriorate as quickly after death as once they did. So report the funeral directors.

Those medical fellows who claim to know say 13 out of every 100 housewives dim down daily with tranquilizers. That's not good.

OPERATING TEMPERATURE

Far more patients survive surgery in the late afternoon than surgery in the early morning. The medicos now know why. Human body temperatures tend to be lowest before dawn, highest before dusk. Bodies are stronger when temperatures are up. Medical statisticians long have known that considerably more surgery patients die between midnight and sunrise than between noon and dusk.

If you don't spend a total of two whole years talking on the telephone during your lifetime, you're just not average.

Certainly don't blame those Pittsburgh lawmakers for ruling it illegal to sleep in a refrigerator.

Q. What's the life span of a robin?

A. Figure 12 years.

HAND BONE'S CONNECTED TO THE . . .

If you're middle-aged, just one of your hands has only about 19 bones in it. But when you were a youngster, it contained 38 bones. It's at about age 18 that those bones start fusing together.

Q. I challenge the claim of those so-called experts who contend that certain trees cause 10 times as much air pollution as man and machine combined. What trees?

A. Pine and sage, say botanists.

POISON

No wonder the questions so frequently arise as to what's poisonous and what's not. Depends on the dosage, almost invariably. There's no absolute line. Too much ordinary table salt can be toxic. A little arsenic can be a medical remedy. All right, maybe some chemicals are so potent they have to be classified as dangerous, even deadly. But most things you can swallow, even water, are both nonpoisonous and poisonous, depending on how much.

The insurance statisticians say most people who live to an extraordinary old age are small in stature.

That Boston shop that specializes in fireplace equipment has a nifty motto: "Everything your hearth desires."

Maybe you know that surgeons now are using staple guns?

Figure your fingernail grows about two inches (5 cm) a year.

Q. Can the radiation in the luminous dial of a watch hurt you?

A. Only if you eat it, my son.

Another reason you ought not eat a monarch butterfly is it's poisonous.

Sodium is poisonous. So is chlorine. Either would knock you flat, if you gobbled up a sufficient supply of one without the other. They don't kill all that many people, though, when combined as common table salt, do they?

OCTOPUS. Nimble critter, the octopus. Marine scientists say they've seen an octopus gather up as many as 25 crabs at one time in its eight arms, then eat them one by one.

BURIAL GROUND

There is a small icy lake in the middle of South Georgia Island in the Antarctic. At the bottom of it are the bodies of countless dead penguins perfectly preserved. Around its shores occasionally are seen droopy penguins obviously sick to near death. Dr. Osmond P. Breland, who reported on the place, said as far as he knew it's the only common burial ground of animals that has ever been discovered.

Was customary in old Rome for mourners at funerals to munch on parsley during the sad orations over the deceased.

BIG BOOM

No doubt you've read of the greatest explosion in history, the volcanic eruption of Krakatoa in the Indian Ocean, where more than 36,000 people were killed. In 1880, that was. Quakes loosened fissures to let sea water through the earth's girdle. And the steam cloud boiled 25 miles (40 km) high while ashes fell over 322,500 square miles (838,500 sq km). Client asks how far away the bang was heard. More than 3,000 miles (4800 km). Think of it this way. If Pike's Peak had blown with the same force, just about everybody in North America who wasn't deaf could have heard the thing clearly.

Item No. 724C in our file labeled "Survival" reads: "If lost in the desert, never take your shoes off. In high heat, it's just about impossible to get them back on. You don't want to try walking through the desert in your bare feet, do you? Certainly not."

Somebody dies violently every 66 seconds.

Approximately one half of those sad souls, who try to commit suicide by shooting themselves through the heart, miss.

It's another little known fact that four out of five suicides don't leave behind explanatory notes.

Have you ever seen that poisonous Upas tree of Java? Neither have I. Report is that its sap is deadly. So deadly, in fact, its drippings will kill any animal that falls asleep under said tree.

KNIFE

During the French Revolution from 1789 through 1793, one guillotine blade, frequently resharpened, beheaded an average of 13 persons a day, month after month, year after year. The most remarkable knife in history, that. It's now in Madame Tussaud's Wax Museum in London. The guillotine scaffold that supported it burned there during a bad fire in 1925.

Death penalty was prescribed in ancient Greece for any man convicted of kissing a woman in a public place, even if said woman were his wife.

A medical man who specializes in circulatory ailments insists: "The world's best cure for swollen feet is a rocking chair."

LONGEVITY

Waiters, bartenders and newspaper reporters do not rank particularly high on the longevity roster. They don't live as long, on the average, as college professors, mathematicians and social workers. In fact, they barely tend to outlive miners, who as a group don't outlive anybody, hardly. Why waiters, bartenders and newspaper reporters seem to survive about equally unwell is not known. But statistics indicate such.

Nuns live longer than women outside the church. On the average. That's also a fact.

When Christopher Columbus made his landing, he wrote a short report about it to the king and queen of Spain, put it in a sealed cedar box, and set it afloat. Exactly 359 years later, the message was found on the shore of Morocco and handed over to officers of the American brig *Chieftain*. Almost 130 years ago. Little late in reporting that. Sorry.

NOSES GROW AND GROW

A doctor of considerable experience says he has never treated a patient 90 years of age or older who didn't have a large nose. But it's not that people with large noses tend to live longer. Other way around. People who live longer tend to develop large noses. Cartilage keeps on growing throughout life.

You can figure it would take the mass of 81 moons to make one earth.

Q. What's a hair's breadth?

A. Exactly? One forty-eighth of an inch (0.52 mm).

Why don't tornadoes hit big cities? Dr. Theodore Fujita thinks he knows the answer to that one. He's a geophysical specialist. The larger towns generate heat that fends off the twisters, he says.

The common cold, flu, pneumonia, those dangerous wheezy ailments most unpoetically referred to as respiratory diseases, do their worst work when the air is dry, not damp. A Dutch researcher named J. H. Hemmes found that out. And a University of Chicago scientist named Dr. Clayton G. Loosli confirmed it. So why have so many physicians for so many years dispatched their lung patients to Arizona? Just to get rid of them, it would seem.

Q. Does anybody know how many sunken ships are on the ocean floor off New England?

A. Estimators say about 4,000, at least. Do you realize more than a million vessels have sunk off coastal waters worldwide in the last 500 years?

Q. Please reprint Channing's famous advice.

A. Gladly. "To live content with small means; to seek elegance rather than luxury, and refinement rather than fashion; to be worthy, not respectable, and wealthy, not rich; to study hard, think quietly, talk gently, act frankly; to listen to stars and birds, to babes and sages, with open heart; to bear all cheerfully, do all bravely, await occasions, hurry never. In a word, to let the spiritual, unbidden and unconscious, grow up through the common. . . ."

The saying goes, "Feed a cold and starve a fever," right? Now, maybe. But originally, it went, "If you stuff a cold, you will have to starve a fever," just the opposite.

What makes the sky blue, daddy? Should your offspring deliver that line, sir, be prepared. The sky is filled with millions of tiny dust particles plus gases. They absorb a lot of the red rays of the sun, but scatter the rays of other colors. And like mixed paint, when those unabsorbed rays combine, they come out blue.

Pedestrians. It's a matter of record, too, that more pedestrians get killed while crossing with the signal than against it.

Remember, sailor, it was Thucydides in the 6th century, B.C., who said, "A collision at sea can ruin your entire day."

She called the Dial-a-Prayer number and was put on hold. She called the Crisis Clinic and got a recording. She called the Unwed Mothers Home and they told her they had a waiting list. She called the Heroin Hotline and an operator said the phone needed fixing. Poor girl. But that's the way it is, isn't it? Goodnight.

Index

Bajau tribe, 258
baker's dozen, 124
baldness, 77, 100, 280
banana, 143, 180, 183, 234; peels, 256
"Bangor tiger," 129
bank guards, 175
bankers, 26
barber, 181-182
Barnum, P.T., 179, 229
bartenders, 302
baseball, 127-128, 131, 132, 135, 136, 137, 138
basketball, 127, 130, 136
Basques, language of, 297
bathing suits, 130-131; *see also* bikinis
baths, 95, 174; rooms, 149-150, 288
bathtubs, 18, 90, 135, 147, 151, 207
bats, food carried by, 253
"Battle Circus," 78
"Battle of Lepanto, The," 64
beach games, 127
bears, 198, 200, 270, 273
beard, 90, 109, 113, 236
bed, 37-38, 88-89; wetting, 275
Bedouins, 89
bees, 140, 141, 150, 201, 225, 261, 265, 282; stings, 255
Belasco, David, 77
Bell, Alexander Graham, 219
Bell, T.H., 174
Bellah, James Warner, 223
Berkshire County Jail, 168
Better Business Bureau, 25
Bible, The, 62, 177, 179
bicycling, 127, 131, 173
bigamist, defined, 186
"bigwig," origin of term, 284
bikinis, 97-98
billboard, 177, 261
billiard ball, 131
Billy the Kid, 220
Bindrim, Paul, 162
birds, 40, 139, 178, 227, 244, 260, 268, 271; *see also* specific birds
birth, 113, 249; *see also* babies
bites, insect, 255
Black Beauty, 62

Blackstone, magician, 67
bladderwort, 232
Blake, Jonathan, 34
Blake, Robert "Baretta," 79
Blarney Stone, 242
blinds, Venetian, 238
blinking, 37
blizzard, 50
blood, 12, 110, 113, 239
Bloomer, Amelia, 12
blondes, 236
"Blue Skin" (horse), 32
blushing, 113
boats, 157
bobcat, 199
body language, 17-18
Bogart, Humphrey, 78, 80
Bonaparte, Napoleon, 11, 215, 218, 285
Bond, James, 57
Bond, Ward, 83
bookies, 100
books, 56-64, 177
Boone, Pat, 72
boots, western, 163, 239
borborygmi, 264
bore, defined, 195
boredom test, 168-169
boric acid powder, 255
boss, origin of word, 116
Bourne, Dr. Geoffrey H., 7
boutiques, 88
bower bird, blue satin, 271
bowleggedness, 111
boxers, 128-129, 134, 135-136, 137
Bradley, General Omar, 62
Brady, Diamond Jim, 23
brain, 44, 112
Brandenberger, Jacques Edwin, 241
bras, 101, 175
brass polish, 254
Brazil, 156; nut, 165
breakfast, 172, 260
breathing, 261
Breland, Osmond P., 301
bricks, 279
bride, price of, 189-190
bridge, stolen, 155
broiling, oven door in, 252
Bronson, Charles, 79, 83

fulgurite, 290
Fulton, Robert, 26
funny bone, 121
Funt, Allen, 72, 78

Gable, Clark, 83
Gale, George Washington, 247
Galsworthy, John, 63
gambling, 35, 56, 69, 90, 96, 99-
    100; see also craps; slot machines
Ganges River, origins of, 55
Garagiola, Joe, 133-134
Garbo, Greta, 80
gardenias, 145
Garland, Judy, 86
garlic, 95-96, 163, 252, 264
garua, 54
Gehrig, Lou, 131
Geminis, 220
generals, 162
genes, 15, 208
genius, fathering, 191
George I, King, 148
Germans, 36, 161, 208, 228
Germany, 7, 151, 286
Geronimo, 32, 283
Gibbs, L., 168
Gibson, Hoot, 84
gila monster, 262
giraffes, 196, 203, 221, 266, 289
glass, 184, 290
goats, 142, 201
Godfrey, Arthur, 62
"God Moves in a Mysterious
    Way . . . ," 74
Goethe, Wolfgang von, 64
gold, 22, 26
goldfish, 234, 271
golf, 127, 130, 134
"Gone With the Wind," 83
goober, origin of word, 142
Goolagong, Evonne, 130
goose, 8, 67, 228, 244, 278;
    Mother, 228
gorillas, 231, 268, 269
Grand Cayman Island, 110
Grant, Ulysses S., 218, 219
"Grape Nuts," 235
grasshoppers, 277
Graziano, Rocky, 85

Gregg, John Robert, 223
Great Lakes, 147
Greece, 7, 11
greetings, 7, 15, 163, 234
greyhound, 208
Grierson, John, 85
Grimm's Fairy Tales, 62
groundhog, 264
"gry," words ending in, 124-125
guillotine blade, 302
guitar, 123, 243
gum ball machines, 97
guppies, 197
gurnard, 231
gymnasium, origin of word, 131
gypsies, 70

hair, 21, 22, 248, 263, 289, 303
"Hallelujah," 116
Hancock, John, 222
hands, 262, 299
handedness, 15, 109, 295
Handel, G.F., 27, 217
handkerchiefs, 257
handshake, 197, 234
handwriting, 285
hangnail, 124
hangovers, 170, 245
Hanshin Park Zoo, 200
happiness, 193
"Happy Days," 23
Harris, Whitley H., 30
Hart, William S., 84
hat, cowboy, 163
hate, synonyms for, 273
Hathaway, Anne, 104
"hatter, mad as a," 61
"Hawaii Five-0," 78
head, human, 17-18, 114; aches,
    93, 109, 156; tipping, 18
health, 93, 94, 95
hearing, peak of, 113
heart, human, 16, 138; attacks, 109
"Hearts of Oak," 77
Heaven, angel in, 210; sailor's, 297
Hebrews, greetings by, 7
height, 227
helicopter, 286
Hemingway, Ernest, 57
Hemmes, J.H., 303
Henry VIII, King, 17

Herold, Don, 257
herring, 180
hiccough fish, 264
hiccups, 66
high heels, 100, 239
"High Noon," 85
highway toll collectors, 175
Hippodrome, 133
hippopotamus, 38, 201, 244, 278
Hitchcock, Alfred, 79
hitchhikers, 180
Hitler, Adolf, 61, 79, 171
hogs, 146, 266, 288, 292; see also
    pigs
hogshead, 118-119
Holland, greetings in, 7
Holmes, Oliver Wendell, 64
home team, 137
Hoover, Herbert, 219
Hoover, J. Edgar, 151
Hope, Bob, 62
horns, loose, 198
horse, 10, 24, 84, 116, 140, 144,
    145, 242, 243, 264, 267; racing,
    134, 135; riding, 127
horseflies, 14
hospitality, Arab, 159
Hotchkiss, James, Jr., 60
hot dog, 33, 239
Hoteiosho, 165
house plants, 253
household hints, 250-259
housewives, 175, 298
Howard, Leslie, 83
Howard, Sidney, 83
Howell, James, 227
Howland, Olin, 83
"Huckleberry Finn," 57
Hudson, Rock, 79
Hudson's Bay, 121
hula, 116
hummingbird, 227, 228
humor, 58, 62
hunger strike, 168
"hungry tigers," 159
hunting, 127, 136, 138
Hurst, Paul, 83
Hutton, Maj. Clayton, 284
hydrogen peroxide, 257
hyperacusia, 262
hypercarinosis, 226

hypertension, 110
hypnophobia, 41
hypnotism, 68
hypochondriacs, 94

ice, thickness of, 53; berg, 53;
    cream, 251; cubes, 256
iced tea, 252
Iceland, 155, 167
"If," 61
illegitimacy, 156
illness, fortune and, 94-95
incest, 192
India, 10, 148, 165
Indians, American, 33, 34, 116,
    118, 181, 280
Indians, Cleveland, 132
indivisibility, 119
infant, meaning of word, 120
Inflation Fighters Club, 23
Ink Spots, 72
insects, 42, 146, 211, 265, 290;
    bites, 255
insomnia, 36, 42, 108
intelligence, 227
Intha tribe, 137
"In the Good Old Summertime,"
    73
"In the Shade of the Old Apple
    Tree," 73
I.O.U., meaning of, 117
Iowa, origin of name, 29
Iranian, ethnicity of, 161
Ireland, 8, 208
Istanbul, Turkey, 174
Italians, 36, 208
Italy, 212, 244
Ivory Soap®, 236
ivy, poison, 180

jaguar, 265
James, Jesse, 32
Japan, 25, 47, 67, 75, 82, 83, 89,
    120, 132, 135, 161, 164, 165,
    244, 246, 291
"Jaws," 84
"Jazz Singer, The," 81
jealousy, 21
Jeanne, Queen, 217
Jefferson, Thomas, 92, 215, 217,
    219, 266, 297

jellyfish, 55, 183
Jesus, 211
jet lag, 286
Jews, 208
Joan of Arc, 37
jobs, 25, 89, 175-176
jokes, 91-92, 126, 172, 247
Jones, Buck, 84
Jones, John Paul, 218
Jordan, Tenneva, 99
judges, 161
Jumbo (elephant), 179
Jung, David, 64
junk food, 118
juries, 152, 153, 176
"Justice," 63
Justinian, Emperor, 188

kangaroos, 16, 91, 120, 137, 201
Kant, Immanuel, 64
Karate, 131
Karlsefni family, 216
Kennedy, John F., 217, 222
key punch operators, 175
Khrushchev, Nikita, 222
"kick the bucket," 297
kid gloves, 119
"King Kong," 79, 86
"King of Hollywood, The," 83
Kiowa Indians, 280
Kipling, Rudyard, 61
"Kiss, The," 82
kissing, 234
Kissinger, Henry, 31, 222
kites, 233
knitting, 17
Knox, Father Ronald A., 62
Knox, Philander, 96
Kohlsaat's Restaurant, 235-236
Kraft Cheese Company, 218
Krakatoa, eruption of, 301
Kremlin, 121-122
Ku Klux Klan, 228

labor union officials, 162
Lamour, Dorothy, 85
land crab, Cuban, 289
Langseth, Hans, 236
languages, 116, 118, 297
Lapuseanu, Alexandru, 195
"Last Chance Gulch," 29

last will and testament, 297-298
latchstring, 123
laundry, 257, 276
laws, 11, 75, 91, 98, 128, 138, 147-
    155, 167, 176, 193, 194, 287,
    288, 291, 299, 302
Lawrence of Arabia, 61
lawsuits, 152-153, 298
lawyers, 161
Lear, Dr. Clement S., 35
Lear, William P., 175-176
Lebanon, 166
Lee, Gypsy Rose, 59
Leigh, Vivian, 83
lemon, 156, 254
Lenin, brain of, 112-113
Leo, 102, 220
leopard, 200, 295
leopons, 200
leppie, 116
Lermontov, Mikhail, 57
letters, 120, 123
lettuce, 250
Levant, Oscar, 188
Lewis, John L., 62
"LGM," 165
Libra, 102, 220
libraries, 56, 58, 84, 86
librocubicularist, 190
licorice flavor, 276
lie detectors, 153-154
life, prime of, 180
"Lifeboat," 79
life span, 179, 182-183
lightning, 46, 173, 182, 288, 293
light switch, 149-150
Lincoln, Abraham, 175, 217, 266
Lincoln, Elmo, 86
linoleum, 256
lions, 196, 199, 200, 201, 203, 204
lip readers, 58
lobster, 239
log birling, 129
long dozen, 124
longevity, 302
long hundred, 124
Longworth, Alice Roosevelt, 247-
    248
loon, 286
Loosli, Clayton G., 303
Lord, Jack, 78

Moore, Lester, 34
Moore, Owen, 34
Moors, greetings by, 7
morons, 183
Moses, 260
mosquitoes, 12, 95-96, 183, 199-200, 255
motels, 151
mothers, 99, 184
Motz, George, 220
mountain climbing, 16
mountains, 53; *see also* specific mountains
moustaches, 100, 172
movies, 79-86, 181, 236
moving, 246
mule, 267
mummies, Egyptian, 41
Munro, H.H., 272
murder, 17, 147, 173, 186
muscles, 104
music, 7, 9, 16, 52, 72-78, 127-128, 261
musicians, 160

nail biting, 265
Namath, Joe, 129, 207
names, 28-34, 159, 238
napkins, asbestos, 166
Narragansett Indians, 22
Nash, Ogden, 22, 187, 269
Nation, Carrie, 216
National Association of Broadcasters, 77
Navy, U.S., superstitions, 66
NBC-TV, 76
Nebraska, meaning of name, 34
needle, sewing, 258
Nepal, advertising in, 88
Nero, 249
nets, spider-web, 166
neuralgia, 93
neurotic, defined, 259
New Guinea, 164, 185, 189-190
Newling, Frederick, 207
Newman, Paul, 82
newsboys, 62, 211
newspaper columnists, 59, 162
newspapermen, 62, 90, 302
Newton, Isaac, 215
New York, 208, 291

nightgowns, 189
"1984," 60
Niven, David, 70, 85
noise, 76, 90, 146, 205
Norway, 8, 159, 160
nose, 90, 167, 209, 234, 259, 303
Notre Dame University, 137, 207
Novich, Max, 114
nudists, 20, 98, 131, 162
number tricks, 25, 70-71
numbers, lucky, 69
Nye, Bill, 7

oak, poison, 180
ocean, 45, 47, 49, 50, 51, 53, 55
ocnophil, 242
octopus, 300
octothorp, 123
Oklahoma, 124
omelet, 251
Onassis, Aristotle, 222
onions, 252
Onion Springs, 49
orange blossoms, 145
Orata, Sergius, 272
Orben, Harold, 188
orchids, 239
orphan, 124, 158
Orr, Mr., 137
Orwell, George, 60
ostrich, 74, 87, 210, 293
Oto Indians, 34
Ouida, 97
ouija board, 69
"Our Gang/Little Rascals," 79
overweight, 12, 43, 72
owls, 172, 208-209, 260
oxygen mask, 129
oysters, 21, 39, 96, 144, 272

Pacific Ocean, 49-50
pain, light and, 210
paint, 257, 262; brushes, 13, 257
pajamas, 36, 99
palindromes, 28, 42, 60-61, 70
palm, greasing of, 275
pandas, giant, 24
panic, uniform and, 280
pantsuit, 98, 189
papain, 255
paperwork, 87

316

redundancies, 60, 63, 209, 237, 248, 252, 272
Reeves, George, 83
reflexes, 224
Reik, Theodor, 14
Renoir, Pierre Auguste, 215
Revere, Paul, 27
rhinoceros, 202, 274
rhubarb, 266
rhyme, unconscious, 60
Richman (scientist), 223
Richthofen, Manfred von, 279
"ring around the rosies . . . ," 39
rings, 149
Riot Act, 148-149
riots, sports, 133
Ritter, Tex, 84
roadrunner, speed of, 289
"roast," 281
robin, life span of, 299
Robinson, Dr. Karl F., 15
Robinson, Edward G., 80
Rochette, Edward, 222
"rockoon," 245
Rocky Mountain spotted fever, 111
rodeo horses, 264
Rogers, Will, 12, 55, 58
"Roget's Thesaurus," 64
roller coasters, 242
roller skating, 114
Romero, Cesar, 81
Roosevelt, Eleanor, 44
Roosevelt, Theodore, 57
roosters, 203
rope trick, Indian, 65
roses, 253, 256
Rostand, Edmond, 209
roulette wheels, 71
Rowan, Henry, 212
runners, long-distance, 44
Russia, *see* U.S.S.R.
Russian roulette, 57
rust, 254

Sagittarian, 70, 220
Sahara Desert, 46
Saint Bernard dog, 52
salary, negotiating, 24
salesmen, 160, 225
salt, 300
Salt Lake City *Deseret News,* 18

San Antonio Carnegie Library, 58
San Salvador, 221
Santa Claus, 165, 178
sauna, 107
"sausage-ism," 239
Sanzenis, Pablo, 40
scallop, eyes of, 209
Scarne, John, 99, 234
Schenley, Ruth S., 184
school teachers, 157
Schuman, Robert, 185
Scorpio, 102, 220
Scotland, 26
Scott, Sir Walter, 59
scream, as burglar alarm, 153
sea, 45, 47-51, 304
seagulls, 67, 213
sea level, 51
seals, 51, 52
seasickness, 246
Seasoned Citizen, 232
Secretariat, 135, 140
secretaries, 157
Secretary of State, 96
seesaw, 248
Segal, Jonathan, 29
seizures, violent, 183
Selim I, Sultan, 7
Sermon on the Mount, 223
Sert, Turks of, 163
sex, 14, 15, 21, 93; differences, 14-21, 25, 27, 39, 43, 99, 113, 114, 138, 188-189, 230, 238, 241, 244, 275, 284; discrimination, 18
"Shadow, The," 218
shaggy dog story, first, 91-92
Shakespeare, William, 30, 104
sharks, 54, 145, 182, 273-274
Shaw, G.B., 210
sheep, 233, 271
"Shell Oil" calculator trick, 212
Sheraton, Thomas, 37-38
ships, sunken, 303
shoelaces, 255
shoes, 114, 180, 214, 253, 277
shoplifters, 150
shopping cart, 181
shorthand, 223
shower, 108
shrew, 225
shrimp, 261, 273

talking, 19, 175
tarantula, 12
taresthesia, 38
tar, 256
Tarzan, 84, 86
tattoos, 98, 152, 161, 241
Taurus, 220
Taveuni, Fiji, 173
taxes, 90
taxi squad, 129
teachers, 162, 249; prejudice, 34
tea leaves, 165, 256
teeth, 108, 161, 163, 199, 211, 269, 282
telegrams, 269
telephone, 166, 219, 296, 299
television, 75-77, 81, 82, 134, 231; news reporters, 162; repairmen, 162
Tell, William, Jr., 220
"Tell it to the marines," 285
temperature, 49, 54, 114, 143, 263
temper, 245
Tennessee Brigade, 285
tennis, 130
Tennyson, Alfred, Lord, 64
terrier, Kerry Blue, 11
tests: boredom, 168-169; color, 171; for normalcy, 263
tethys snail, 269
Texas, 291
Thailand, 161
Thalberg, Irving, 224
thermometer, 253
thirst, 110-111
Thomas, Danny, 188
Thomas, Norman, 44
throat, sore, 213
Thucydides, 304
thumb, 166
thunder, 66; cloud, 47
tickets, traffic, 184, 292
Tierra Del Fuego, 20
tigers, 55, 199, 200, 262
tiger rag, 115-116
tiger's milk, 252
tightrope walker, 76
Tilzer, Albert von, 76
Titian, 64
toads, 144
Tolstoy, Leo, 58

"Tom Sawyer," 61
tongue twisters, 8, 226
tornadoes, 46, 48, 303
Toronto, origin of name, 125
tourists, Japanese, 164, 282
Tracy, Spencer, 82
train, 10, 291; conductor, 246
tranquilizers, 298
travel bureaus, 160
travelers' checks, 153
Treasure Island, 62
trees, 38, 46, 93, 140, 146, 299, 302
Tripoli, Libya, 209
Truman, Harry S., 62
truth, 161-162
turkeys, 227
Turner, Lana, 83
turnpike, origin of, 291
turtles, 139, 293
TV dinner, 25
Twain, Mark, 13, 55, 57, 61, 62, 96, 118, 209
twins, 9, 30, 109, 191
"tycoon," origin of word, 280-281
typewriter, 56
typing, 104, 175
Tyrannosaurus, 85

"u," letter, 123
"U boats," 286
Ulan Bator, Mongolia, 52
umpires, 134-135
Uncle Sam, 236
"Uncorker of Ocean Bottles," 149
undertakers, 295, 298
Urban, Dr. Yinder, 65
U.S.A., 75, 83, 152, 154, 156, 159, 160, 173, 180, 181, 185, 219, 228, 246, 285, 291
U.S.S.R., 8, 15, 24, 52, 228
used car salesmen, 161

Vance, Philo, 58
Vanda, Lake, 47
Van Dine, S.S., 58
vanilla, natural, 146
Vaseline®, 92
vegetables, canned, 245
vegetarians, 58, 139, 142, 166, 184

319

vehicle, first, 163
veil, bridal, 188
veins, varicose, 92
ventriloquism, meaning of word,
 73
Verdi, Giuseppe, 64
Vermont, 294
Victoria, Queen, 207, 275
Vikings, 54
vinegar, 257
violin and violinists, 77, 245
Virgo, 106, 220
vocabulary, 121, 160, 292
volcanoes, 47
Volta, Count, 216
Voltaire, Francois Marie Arouet,
 90-91

Wade, Harry V., 59
Wagner, Richard, 7
waiters, 257, 302
waitresses, 131, 105
"Wait Till the Sun Shines, Nellie,"
 73
Walker, Clint, 82
walking, 52, 183
"Want to buy a duck?," 77
wars, 279, 282, 283, 285, 286
Warner, Charles Dudley, 55
warts, 16
Washington, George, 32, 57, 163
Washington, Martha, 130-131
Washington Monument, 219
washroom, 288
wasps, 262
watchdial, 300
watchmakers, 245
water, 47, 49, 50
Waterloo, 215
Watchtower, 60
Waterman, Dr. Norton G., 23
watermelon, 141-142
waves, travel speed of, 49
Wayne, John, 85
weather, 45-55, 66, 294; prediction,
 67, 70, 140
Weaver, Dennis, 82
weddings, 182
Weems, Parson, 57
weight, body, 101-102, 111, 112,
 268; lifting, 130
Wellington, Duke of, 215

Westfall, Wendy, 23
whales, 24, 30, 40, 53, 99, 121,
 150-151, 225, 243, 290
Whewell, William, 60
whiskey, 121
Whistler's Mother, 28
White, E.B., 241
"white eyes," 181
White Flash (horse), 84
Whitey (horse), 84
wicker, longevity of, 254
wigs, 281-282
Wilde, Oscar, 195
Winchell, Walter, 59
windmills, 26
wine glass, 214
Winkler, Henry, 23
Winnie the Pooh, 62
wise men, nativity, 179
witches, 65, 70, 170
"Wizard of Oz, The," 86
Wolfe, Thomas, 61
wolves, 9, 197, 228
women, 18-19, 21, 37, 81, 97, 98-
 106, 185
wood, petrified, 143
words, 115-125
work, 114, 262
World Wars, 23, 170, 283, 286
wormwood, 121
worry, 171
wrestling, 128
Wright, Willard Huntingdon, 58
Wrigley, William, Jr., 25-26
wrinkles, 104, 106
writers, 56-64, 90, 160
Wurstigkeit, 239

Yahgan Indians, 20
yaks, 10
Yellow Pages, 66
Yerkes Primate Research Center, 7
Young, Brigham, 218
yoyos, 45

zebras, 37
Zela, Battle of, 286
Zelazo, Philip R., 111
zippers, 254
zoonoses, 276
zoos, 197-198, 271